THEY'RE DRIVING ME MAD!

Jenny Mosley and Zara Niwano

Permission to photocopy

This book contains materials which may be reproduced by photocopier or other means for use by the purchaser. The permission is granted on the understanding that these copies will be used within the educational establishment of the purchaser. The book and all its contents remain copyright. Copies may be made without reference to the publisher or the licensing scheme for the making of photocopies operated by the Publishers' Licensing Agency.

The rights of Jenny Mosley and Zara Niwano to be identified as the authors of this work have been asserted by them in accordance with sections 77 and 78 of the Copyright, Designs and Patents Act 1988.

MT10171
ISBN-13: 978 1 85503 423 5
© Jenny Mosley and Zara Niwano
Illustrations © Mark Cripps
First published 2007

Printed in the UK for LDA
Abbeygate House, East Road, Cambridge, CB1 1DB, UK

Acknowledgements

We should like to thank all of the following for their contribution to this book:

Ross Grogan, who is always full of ideas and common sense. We have turned to her many times during the writing of this book.

Jean Gross, who gave us lots of encouragement and support during her time as the director of the DfES Social and Emotional Aspects of Learning programme.

David Moore, HMI, who showed great interest in Quality Circle Time in its early stages and still does so today.

The Social, Emotional and Behavioural Difficulties Association (SEBDA) for their pioneering work under the leadership of Ted Cole and Joan Pritchard. SEBDA hold exciting conferences and support wide-ranging research projects in this field.

The office team at Jenny Mosley Consultancies. Despite being very busy, they have given us support whenever we have needed it. Our special thanks to Ginny Sutton, who for many years has shown patience, creativity and the ability to multi-task.

Jayne Allan, Simon Bishop, Anne Crease, Maggie Dent, Penelope Moon, Helen Sonnet, Carol Trower, Shannon Woolf, and the Massage in Schools Programme Committee – all of whom kindly wrote about aspects of their work.

Marion Bennathon and her vision of emotionally healthy children.

We should like to acknowledge our appreciation of Corin Redsell for his work and vision in untiringly bringing to fruition this book and many others for teachers.

Rebecca Goodbourne of the Campaign for Learning; Ben Wye, Amanda Hart, Matt Perrett, Fizz Starkey and Kate Wall of the Centre for Learning and Teaching, Newcastle University; and Janet White for their support.

The Leigh Park Hotel, Bradford-on-Avon, and all its staff for the friendly atmosphere and amazing service that they provide.

Contents

Foreword

This approachable and heart-felt book is a welcome addition to Jenny Mosley and her colleagues' list of useful publications. It relates the theory and practice of Circle Time to the agenda of Social and Emotional Aspects of Learning (SEAL) and Every Child Matters. It describes the extension of Circle Time practice for use with challenging children and young people who need the more intensive support offered by Wave 2 of SEAL.

The book's messages are very much in line with the long-held beliefs of the Social Emotional and Behavioural Difficulties Association (SEBDA), which have informed the professional development days and training courses we have offered to workers in the field over the last fifty years. Wave 1 of SEAL is crucial. However, teachers, teaching assistants, mentors and others working with children need time and inclination to look beyond the outward display of challenging behaviour to understand and empathise with the child within. Recognising and responding to social and emotional underpinnings are essential for improved behaviour in the classroom in order to make contact and to make crucial relationships with those Jenny and Zara describe as the children 'beyond'. Listening, understanding and empathising with children through circles of support is a valuable approach, helping the inclusion of some of the children who are hard to reach.

As SEBDA has long argued, inclusion cannot be imposed by well-meaning outsiders. The danger is that it can be a hollow form of human rights in its practical manifestation. Inclusion is only a meaningful concept if it is felt by the child – if the child or young person feels they are valued and belong. Whether this happens in a mainstream, special or alternative setting is a secondary issue. Application of the messages from this book is, however, likely to increase the chances of more real inclusion in mainstream schooling. The book contains an attractive reminder of timeless and time-tested theory, as well as offering highly practical advice on running successful small circles of support. It also introduces the reader to the potential of other useful holistic approaches for those with the most challenging of needs.

Dr Ted Cole, Executive Director, SEBDA

Preface

'They're driving me mad' is a politically incorrect statement. However, often we speak and act in ways that we wish we hadn't in response to the behaviour of children who are beyond what normally works in the classroom. Sometimes we shout or shred a child's reputation in the staffroom, and sometimes we hold on to our confusion, hurt and anger – only to moan to our families or friends later.

I started teaching in a secondary modern boys' school. My class, 15 years old, thought they were just about to leave school. Then they were hit by the Raising of the School Leaving Age Act 1972, which stated that they had to continue until they were 16. Anger and despair abounded. Some of their mates, by virtue of their mothers' labour pains being earlier, were able to leave school and try to get a job. A number of them couldn't and spent their time driving round our leaking mobile classroom on their mopeds, giving us the two-finger sign as they went by. For me, as a probationary English teacher, it was sink or swim. I sought out enjoyable activities to try to hold the class's attention. I used drama, role play and games, and I brought in local artists and musicians. Conflict and anger diminished, and we became a tighter knit, higher-achieving group.

As a result I became very interested in working with troubled children, and I went to teach in an EBD school in Clapham Junction. At the same time I was studying to become a drama therapist. My experiences as a therapist and a teacher in special and mainstream education taught me that these areas have 'relationship' as their unifying bond. However, the framework within which you promote genuine and accepting relationships needs to be different. As a young teacher and drama therapist, I believed passionately in the value of the arts and experiential learning to build self-esteem. This, however, created a degree of mayhem and chaos.

Later, I learnt – amongst other things – the value of shared, established boundaries for groups and agreed consequences, and I learnt there was a need to focus on an issue and not get personal. I realised that therapy can be educational and education can be therapeutic. I also realised that I needed a clear understanding of both, otherwise I would jeopardise the clarity and emotional safety that are at the heart of the process for young people. In time, I went on to teach creative arts in therapy and education on a master's course for twelve years and started my own company to promote Quality Circle Time for all children.

Here I am today, co-writing a book that advocates the running of small therapeutic circles for children beyond the usual motivational strategies. I first started work in this area in 1986. In 1988 I wrote an article based on my research involving small circles of support (Mosley 1988). The article advocated that mainstream schools should adopt this approach. Nearly two decades later I am still championing the same theory. Many things have changed for the better, but the plight of severely troubled children has got worse. There are many more of them and there is far less support than ever before.

The DfES Social and Emotional Aspects of Learning (SEAL) materials promote the three-waves approach to help teachers support their children. Wave 1 is about establishing a positive, proactive ethos for learning. Wave 2, the primary focus of this book, aims to help schools to bring troubled children back into the fold. Lastly, Wave 3 is concerned with preparing individualised programmes of support. Wave 4 does not exist, and that is a tragic injustice. Some deeply unhappy children need temporary respite or full-time relief from their home situations. They need to be cared for in a therapeutic community consisting of a range of workers – teachers, psychiatrists, arts therapists, social workers and others.

Unlike in the 1970s and 1980s, very few of these communities exist today because they are considered too costly. This is short-term thinking. The cost to society of not responding to such children's needs could be very high indeed.

We are very happy to present this book to you. We believe that the setting up of circles of support for troubled children, if done properly, is vital. Our hope is that Wave 4 will appear before much more time has passed.

Jenny Mosley

Introduction

An ordinary Tuesday morning, 9.00 a.m.

It was morning registration for Year 2. Joe refused to sit at his table and shouted out that he wanted to do some colouring. A teaching assistant (TA) tried to talk to him, but he yelled back and dashed across the room. He banged a cupboard door, yelling all the time. The TA tried some gentle distraction techniques, but Joe was not fooled by them and threw a chair across the room. The teacher put down the register, ready to approach the child since his behaviour was clearly dangerous to himself and others. As the teacher walked towards him, Joe pushed past and ran out of the room. The teacher followed Joe, and the TA finished taking the register. By now most of the children were agitated and unable to sit and listen quietly.

9.20 a.m.
The teacher returned and had to raise his voice to regain the children's attention. The TA went to support the headteacher, who was dealing with Joe.

Witnessed at a mainstream primary school

The problem

Some children may appear to be beyond the strategies that you have put in place for positive classroom ethos and sound behaviour management. These are the children who may drive you to distraction, press all your emotional crumple buttons and metaphorically force you into a corner. They may distort your sense of perspective, destroy your good humour and drain your energy. These children are often expert at this sort of behaviour – so expert that other children, their neighbours and even their parents or carers are wary of them. The children themselves are often aware of this, which may confirm their view that they are unlovable and capable only of hurting others. Such children need to discover:

☀ a sense of self-worth;
☀ control over their behaviour and actions;
☀ a positive self-image.

They also need to be given:

☀ a guarantee of some success in life;
☀ some therapeutic time within school.

Their teachers need to be given the same opportunities.

Who is this book for?

This book is written for mainstream primary school practitioners: headteachers, deputy heads, teachers, TAs, SENCos, learning mentors, behaviour support workers – in fact, anyone who works with children who push them to their limits. The session plans can be used as they are or adapted to suit younger or older children.

The main aim of this book

This book's main aim is to provide guidance on what to do when the positive behaviour systems in the classroom fail to meet the needs of certain children. We describe these children as being beyond the current systems, but not beyond hope or help. The guidance includes a system called circles of support and offers detailed session plans for such circles. In addition, we shall share with you some examples of projects that we have encountered to help children who are beyond the usual systems.

The book also offers a number of checklists that will help you to assess your school's policy for positive behaviour.

What can this book do for you?

This book provides strategies, advice and resources to help you address the challenges that you face with the children you teach. For these things to be effective, certain general systems of support should be in place. It is valid to say that a child is beyond all systems only if the systems are consistently and coherently embedded in the life of the school and are not working. These systems should incorporate whole-school values and rules, and policies for children's emotional and social development, incentives and sanctions, and lunchtime behaviour.

However, there are no miracle cures. For some children classroom strategies and therapeutic support within school will not be enough to counterbalance the unhappiness, anger and insecurities that they have accumulated. This book is not a substitute for professional help for children suffering with severe problems. It should not replace specialised training to deal with the severe individual needs of children within your care.

Is there really light at the end of the tunnel?

Yes, sometimes. We have found that careful and consistent support may encourage children back into the fold, especially those on the brink of going beyond and those needing further intervention. It may also prevent some children heading towards beyond.

While writing this book it became apparent that most of the chapters could be expanded into books. Some other areas are beyond the scope of the book. We have thought hard about the areas we have explored or not explored, and inevitably we have omitted some and gone into less detail with others. What we have tried to do is to allow you to take several steps forward in your professional practice and deepen your understanding and management of children beyond the usual strategies.

1 What is happening in schools?

All over the country dedicated and creative teachers are being put to the test. At best we could say they are challenged, and at worst thwarted, in their struggle to present a balanced curriculum to their children calmly and effectively. The individual needs and resultant behaviour of a minority of children may overwhelm their plans.

Well-prepared lessons are frequently sabotaged, leaving teachers and children feeling hurt and frustrated rather than nurtured and inspired. Instead of enjoying the positivity that comes from working alongside children, teachers are likely to go home weary and angry.

> *With as many as one in five children experiencing psychological problems at any one time, primary schools across the UK should be doing more to identify and support children at risk of developing mental health problems.*
>
> Mental Health Foundation, June 2001

Is this behaviour new and can we do something to help?

Challenging behaviour has always been part of school life, but it sometimes feels as if a greater degree of challenge exists today than ever before. Children who consistently behave unpredictably, dangerously or disruptively are a hazard to themselves and affect the emotional, psychological and physical well-being of others. Such children will not learn sufficiently and are a worry to all who are involved with them.

A child who is disempowered by life may seize back power by disempowering others.

There are many theories about why this situation exists. Some emphasise the changing nature of the family unit and the challenges this presents. Others point to the increasingly electronically led nature of childhood, the growth of materialism and changes in the workplace. Whatever the reason(s), the impact of challenging behaviour on the morale and self-esteem of those involved in teaching is enormous. When we discuss this matter with teachers, they list children who have the following attributes as giving them the most concern:

- ⋇ self-hate;
- ⋇ violence and risk of hurting themselves and others;
- ⋇ lack of awareness of the extremes of their behaviour;
- ⋇ withdrawn and disengaged manner;
- ⋇ inability to make eye contact;
- ⋇ disruptive and attention-seeking behaviour;
- ⋇ compulsive, repetitive and potentially obsessive behaviour.

Teachers are working harder than ever and often receiving first-class training, but this situation distresses us all. In addition, many teachers are exhausted by the struggles they face, and are experiencing increasing stress levels. We offer a checklist on page 14 to help you begin to find the way out of this situation. The good news is that the following steps can minimise such problems:

WILL THIS BE THE FINAL STRAW?

- ⋇ support children with proactive strategies to prevent their going beyond;
- ⋇ use strategies and systems to reinforce boundaries, providing safety and security;
- ⋇ regularly celebrate positive behaviour so that it is accepted and enjoyed as the norm;
- ⋇ use psychologically proven techniques to help children 'beyond' take positive steps forward;
- ⋇ support and listen to staff within school so that nobody feels isolated;
- ⋇ create an open forum in which children share their feelings about school situations;
- ⋇ enlist the help of other staff to manage the school day;
- ⋇ seek professional support and advice to help children with their needs.

These suggestions will help you to manage those children who are beyond the usual strategies effectively and appropriately. They will help to eliminate the most disruptive behaviour so that classroom life becomes more peaceful and more like the creative and effective learning environment that it is supposed to be.

Unfortunately, not all children are able to respond to such techniques. They are beyond the scope of this book. They will need therapeutic support to move forward. Our recommendation would be early professional intervention to give them the greatest opportunities that are available to them.

> *The only person who is educated is the one who has learned how to learn and change.*
>
> Carl Rogers, founder of Person-centred Therapy

Key points

★ A minority of children have social, emotional and behavioural needs that are beyond the norm. Their difficulties may mean they disrupt lessons, leaving others unable to engage with constructive learning.

★ Primary schools need to address the needs of children with psychological problems and help prevent other children from developing similar difficulties.

★ Poor behaviour has an impact on staff morale and self-esteem. The Government recognises this and has set up initiatives to address the areas of behaviour, attendance, and social and emotional aspects of learning.

★ Two-thirds of 230 teachers questioned by the BBC in 2004 said that problems with discipline were preventing them from doing their job properly.

★ Skills and techniques for dealing effectively and appropriately with children beyond the reach of usual classroom strategies can be learnt. These can raise teachers' energy levels and help the children in their care.

When teaching is getting you down

	Yes	No
Can you honestly say that a child's behaviour is not exacerbated by the way you teach? Is the curriculum differentiated? Do all the children in your class experience success?		
Could you suggest a Circle Time for staff at which issues concerning children 'beyond' can be raised?		
Would you be brave enough to ask for help and admit that a child is seriously threatening the emotional health of both you and your class?		
Could you suggest, or accept if it is for yourself, a timetable of support created by the staff? This might involve members of staff offering an hour or so each day to invite a child you are having difficulty with into their classroom.		
Would you be prepared to invite a troubled child into your classroom to give a colleague some respite?		
Can you accept that it may not be you, your colleagues or your school that has failed a child? It may be the mainstream system that is failing the troubled child. They may need more limited boundaries and positive contacts to make life safer and happier for them.		
During a stressful period, can you step up your personal care plan in order to replenish your energy? Only if you care for yourself physically and create moments of fun will you keep a positive perspective on life.		
Can you remember that a troubled child does not encapsulate the whole of your teaching career?		
Can you remind other teachers that an unhappy child requires a whole-school response?		

2 Who are children 'beyond'?

What do we mean by 'beyond'?

We use the term children 'beyond' in a specific way. We are not describing children as beyond hope or help. We mean children who are beyond the reach of the usual motivational strategies that we promote through the Quality Circle Time (QCT) model – the support and facilitation that are found in caring and well-organised schools.

The demand for training linked to QCT over the last twenty years has taken us all over the UK and abroad. Thousands of schools have now embedded the QCT model into their practice and the DfES has consistently recommended our approach. Our time in schools enables us to gauge how teachers are feeling and to recognise where the real challenges lie.

Increasingly, teachers insist that they have a small group of children who are beyond their classroom systems. These children have the potential to create chaos. For the sake of these children and the sanity of the adults working with them, we need to ensure that effective and supportive systems are functioning in the classroom.

The table on page 21, although not exhaustive, will help you to assess whether a child is unhappy. If the child is demonstrating a range of the behaviours listed and not responding to any proactive classroom systems, then we may well consider them to be beyond. SEAL refers to such children as 'Wave 2 children'.

Light-bulb moments

We all have our own light-bulb moments in our careers as educators. For me such a moment was when I began to understand that there are three very different reasons for children not behaving as we want them to. One reason is that they have not yet learnt the skills that underpin positive and pro-social behaviour. Another is that they have the skills but are choosing not to use them because alternative choices offer them bigger pay-offs. A third reason is that, although they have the skills and although the incentives to use those skills are in place, they are simply too hurt and distressed to make wise choices.

QCT was another light-bulb moment for me. It seemed a magic way of addressing all three of the possible reasons for behaviour difficulties. The framework of Golden Rules and Golden Time, explained in Better Behaviour through Golden Time *(see the books and resources in Chapter 13), provides the motivation. Circle sessions teach the skills children need in order to manage their feelings, develop empathy, and make and keep friends. The sessions also provide the kind of nurturing environment that reduces children's distress and hurt by enabling them to share their feelings with others and receive support.*

That is why Circle Time is important in the Government's approach to the social and emotional aspects of learning materials (SEAL), on which I was privileged to work. More and more teachers are using Circle Time routinely in their classrooms, and looking for guidance and support in how to use it well.

Jean Gross, Director of SEAL,

in Jenny Mosley, *Step by Step*, Positive Press, 2006

A brief introduction to SEAL and its three-wave model

In 2005 the DfES published its SEAL materials, which aimed to provide a creative and structured framework for developing children's social, emotional and behavioural skills. QCT is featured in this document as 'a highly effective approach for the delivery of the SEAL curriculum'. The social and emotional aspects of learning described in this resource are self-awareness, managing feelings, motivation, empathy and social skills.

There are three waves of support mentioned in SEAL:

Wave 1: Described as 'quality first teaching of social, emotional and behavioural skills to all children; effective whole-school or setting policies and frameworks for promoting emotional health and wellbeing'.

Wave 2: Described as 'small-group intervention for children who need additional help in developing skills, and for their families'.

Wave 3: Described as 'additional highly personalised interventions'.

When we talk about children 'beyond', we mean those children at Wave 2 of the SEAL strategies.

QCT is the model used in this book. Like SEAL it uses a waves-of-support model. Both models provide increasingly supportive levels of assistance for children who need it most.

The QCT model, described in further detail in Appendix 1 (page 162), includes the following waves.

Wave 1 – positive, proactive, behavioural support for everyone

This wave includes:

- ✳ strategies to boost the self-esteem and morale of all adults;
- ✳ a moral values code, or Golden Rules;
- ✳ an incentives and sanctions system called Golden Time;
- ✳ a system of tiny, achievable, tickable targets to help struggling children;
- ✳ school-wide listening systems, including class Circle Time;
- ✳ a one-to-one listening system called Bubble Time;
- ✳ Think Time Books for children to use to write down how they are feeling;
- ✳ a positive playtime policy.

As this level of support is critical for all children, we have included brief descriptions and checklists in Appendix 1 to help you ensure that these systems are in place in your school. See Chapter 13 for further reading.

Wave 2 – circles of support for children 'beyond' and other small-group work

If a child does not respond to the systems of Wave 1, they will require the small-group work of Wave 2. We call this a 'Circle of Support'. A Circle of Support is a small group of carefully chosen children, who meet for a number of sessions designed to focus on social, emotional and behavioural skills. This is the main focus of this book.

In 2006 the DfES published some supplementary guidance on the use of small groups in Key Stage 2. This is a silver coloured set of booklets. The programme described in the guidance is designed to help those children who have not responded to Wave-1 systems. The Circle of Support programme we advocate has the same aims as this guidance.

A checklist to help you decide if a child is beyond the usual motivational strategies may be found on page 21.

Wave 3 – therapeutic, intensive support for children 'beyond'

For children who need more than Wave 2, further support should be available. When all else fails, children will need to be referred to trained therapists. Wave 3 might include intensive behaviour support, psychotherapy, drama and art therapy. We outline some thoughts on such therapeutic approaches in Appendix 2. These practices will help to make the inner world of the child 'beyond' clearer to them and to those who are working with them.

Children who need Wave 2 or 3 support are likely to have felt emotionally unsafe when younger. For these children the hidden message from their early experiences is that being out of control is terrifying. The only way to gain any control is not to care. Hence they might rip up their work if they are praised for it or run out of the hall if they are thanked in assembly. Success can be terrifying as it generates feelings of hope, which means that they might look forward to

BY NEVER HOPING YOU DON'T RISK BEING DISAPPOINTED.

seeing again the person who praised them. If they accept praise, they may think that they need to perform at this level all the time and they are not sure they can. They may feel that it was a fluke the first time anyway. Failure can be seductive. It may appear that if you make no effort no one will expect anything of you or give anything to you, and so you cannot let anyone down.

In other words, it means that you become in control of your world once more. By never hoping you don't risk being disappointed. To achieve this, positive feelings would have to be rejected. All good relationships would need to be damaged. All praiseworthy work must be destroyed. Failure can become addictive.

There is a danger that as teachers we may become co-dependents in this addiction. A teacher may become defeated by the rejection and public humiliation they experience when dealing with such a child. As a result their self-esteem becomes low. They may have no supervision and nobody to talk to – apart from family or friends who may be bored with their complaints. This can lead to the teacher acting like the child, pretending they don't care, labelling the child 'a waste of space', insulting them to other staff, and picking on them in the classroom. By this behaviour the teacher confirms the child's view that they are useless and deserve rejection.

A word of warning

Sometimes the ways in which schools establish their behaviour systems can be so lacking in thought, so poor in their theoretical grounding, that children experience the flaws or weaknesses at first hand. A child in danger of going beyond will feel unsafe and may try to play one adult against another in order to create their own sense of continuity and unity.

This is the danger with establishing ill-thought-through circles of support. If a school sets up such groups but fails to provide a system of communication between the group and the relevant staff, problems will occur. For example a child may view the Circle of Support facilitator as an ally and the class teacher as the enemy. This can add to the fragmentation of a child's psyche.

This book describes a system of circles of support that features clear channels of communication.

Key points

★ We use children 'beyond' to mean those children beyond the reach of the motivational strategies that we promote through the QCT model, or children beyond Wave 1 of SEAL.

★ By Wave 1 of QCT we mean positive, proactive behavioural support for everyone – including a system of boundaries, incentives and sanctions, lunchtimes and playtimes policies and a small-target system for children who find the incentives system for the majority too difficult.

★ By Wave 2 of QCT we mean circles of support which offer specific small-group work for children 'beyond'.

★ By Wave 3 of QCT we mean intensive, therapeutic support for children.

★ There are numerous reasons why some children are beyond the systems of Wave 1 of QCT. To help with this, it is important to try to understand what a child's inner-world experience may be like.

★ Care is needed when setting up any support or intervention for children 'beyond' to ensure it does not create further problems for the child.

A guide to whether a child may be beyond the usual motivational strategies

The child regularly . . .	exhibits this behaviour	Tick if applicable
seeks attention	makes a lot of noise, shouts out	
doesn't do as they are asked	does the opposite	
can't/won't communicate properly	lashes out, winds people up, won't speak	
can't/won't settle properly	bothers other children, rushes round the room	
has low personal expectations	tearful, doesn't try, gives up easily	
has little self-confidence	puts themselves down	
demonstrates poor pupil–pupil and staff–pupil relationships	cannot engage in sustained conversation	
has mood swings	cheerful one moment, angry the next	
experiences feelings of being unwell	says they feel sick, poor attendance, asks to go home	
is a bolter	runs out of the room at the first opportunity	
becomes reliant upon certain staff	clings on, follows staff member	
shows lack of eye contact	looks down or away	
has lack of personal awareness	clumsy, pushes others	
has temper tantrums	destroys work or resources	
acts in ways that may hurt themselves	acts in a reckless manner without thinking	
is withdrawn	is verbally reticent, consistently says 'Pass' in Circle Time, never volunteers an answer	
disrupts the lesson	distracts others, never has the right equipment	
disregards people's feelings, bodies and property	scribbles on tables, drops litter, pushes people out of the way	
avoids the truth	tells lies, hides things	
has low self-esteem	will not try new things, hates any challenge, avoids new situations	
attempts to cover up their difficulties	may be loud, shouts out answers	
has trigger points – once one thing goes slightly wrong, everything else is wrong too	gets in a mood or temper if someone answers before them	
shows loner behaviour	inability to join in games and group activities	
has poor concentration	doesn't finish work; does a hasty, slapdash job	
risks hurting others, does not take care	plays dangerously	
has poor resilience	gives up on a task, self, people or game easily	

3 Linking waves of support and educational thinking

In this chapter we shall explain briefly how a range of educational theories and governmental strategies support and underpin Wave 1 and 2 of QCT described in Chapter 2.

On page 26 there is a table that indicates how the following approaches are reflected in QCT. It is important that the work we do with children as part of Wave 1 and 2 of QCT builds on shared strategies and common goals that are underpinned by theory and practice.

Every Child Matters

The aim of *Every Child Matters* (DfES 2003a) is to ensure that every child has the opportunity to fulfil their potential by focusing on the following five outcomes:

- **S** – staying safe;
- **H** – being healthy;
- **A** – achieving and enjoying;
- **P** – making a positive contribution;
- **E** – economic well-being.

Wave 1 of QCT provides proactive boundaries for physical and emotional safety, incentives for social, emotional and behavioural achievement, and three listening systems for cohesion and communication. These systems address the five outcomes. However, children beyond Wave 1 of QCT will need extra support in order for them to access their right to fulfil their potential.

> *Children learn better when they are excited and engaged. What excites and engages them best is truly excellent teaching which challenges them and shows them what they can do. When there is joy in what they are doing, they learn to love learning.*
>
> DfES 2003b

A child's unrecognised emotional and social needs may prevent them from enjoying school and feeling a sense of achievement. Helping such a child is a crucial step towards reducing their educational failure, and improving the child's pro-social behaviour and emotional health.

Using circles of support is a recognition of the additional support that some children need to engage with and enjoy learning. The learning of skills and social opportunities found within the

WHERE THERE IS JOY IN WHAT THEY ARE DOING, CHILDREN LEARN TO LOVE LEARNING.

circles is based on using enjoyable and engaging activities to connect children 'beyond' with other children and the adult facilitator(s). This happens while opportunities for emotional and social growth and development are systematically introduced.

The wave model and Maslow's hierarchy of human needs

First published in *Motivation and Personality* (1954), Abraham Maslow's hierarchy ranks the human needs that provide us with our motivation for living. Although it has been updated, the original model remains the definitive version for many people.

The needs that Maslow describes are as follows:

1. Biological and physiological needs – e.g. air, food, drink, shelter, warmth, sleep.

2. Physical and emotional safety needs – e.g. security, order, law, limits, stability, boundaries, predictable safe consequences.
3. Belongingness and love needs – e.g. group work, family, affection, relationships.
4. Esteem needs – e.g. self-esteem, achievement, mastery, independence, status, acclaim, prestige.
5. Self-actualisation needs – e.g. realising personal potential, self-fulfilment, seeking personal growth, peak experiences.

The model advocates satisfying each need in turn, starting with the first level. Only when the lower-order needs are satisfied can a person be concerned with the higher ones. If the things that satisfy lower-order needs are swept away, a person is generally no longer concerned about the maintenance of their higher-order needs.

According to Maslow's model, the need for physical and emotional safety follows the need for air, food, drink, shelter, warmth and sleep. In other words, all these are fundamental needs. Children will do whatever is required, however negative, to gain some semblance of safety.

For most children, Wave-1 systems will help with physical and emotional safety in school, and with their belonging and self-esteem needs. For other children, Wave-2 or Wave-3 initiatives may be needed too.

> *I know a child in my class who has no gas or electricity at home. In winter he and his brother say that they do not eat proper meals at home, just crisps and snacks from a local shop. Their clothes are unwashed and they are embarrassed by their appearance. As the year has progressed, I have noticed the child become more withdrawn and less able to cope and participate. I feel powerless and do not know how to help.*
>
> Year 3 teacher, 2006

Emotional intelligence

In 1983 Howard Gardner published his claim that there is more than one form of intelligence – notably for this book, interpersonal and intrapersonal intelligences.

In 1996 *Emotional Intelligence* by Daniel Goleman was published. Significantly, Goleman suggested that emotional intelligence competencies are not innate talents but learned abilities. If this is the case, we can offer children opportunities to develop competencies and learn the skills associated with the different intelligences. However, as with academic subjects, some children will need a differentiated emotional curriculum to access and implement the abilities.

Key points

★ The waves of support within QCT are reflected in current practice and educational theories.

★ Every Child Matters seeks to ensure that all children have the opportunity to fulfil their potential – a concept supported by our circles of support model.

★ Like the SEAL resources, circles of support help children with additional needs to develop social, emotional and behavioural skills.

★ Maslow's hierarchy of human needs stresses the need for physical and emotional safety, and for love and belonging – circles of support address such needs.

★ Daniel Goleman recognised that emotional intelligence competencies are learned abilities that can be taught. Children can benefit from this knowledge, and from activities to help develop these skills.

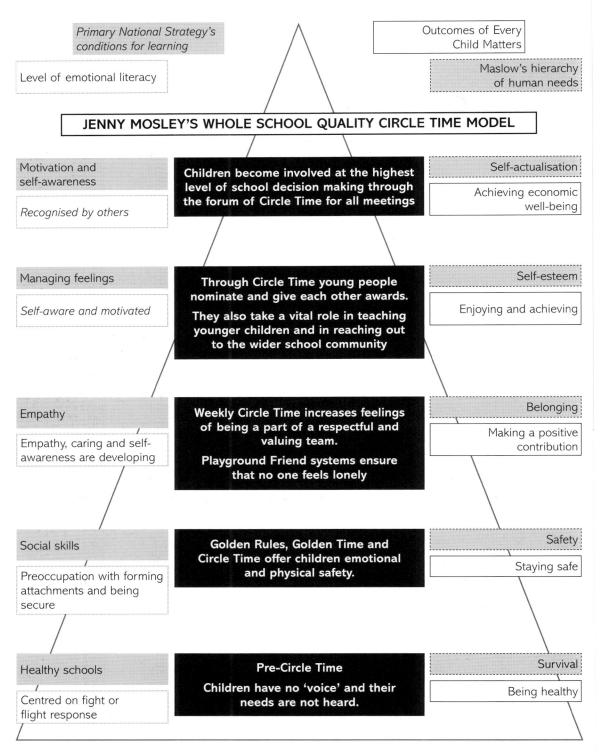

Compiled with the support of Janet White and other trainers who attend Jenny Mosley's Accredited Quality Circle Time Train the Trainers course

4 Introducing circles of support for children 'beyond'

What is a Circle of Support?

A Circle of Support is an early intervention strategy for children who are not responding to Wave 1. These are the key features of a Circle of Support:

- ☀ A group will consist of four to six children 'beyond' and up to four children with good social and behavioural skills who will benefit from small-group work.
- ☀ Each child should be interviewed first and asked if they are happy to participate.
- ☀ A Circle of Support functions best with two adult facilitators, who are allowed time to plan and review sessions.
- ☀ The group should meet in a quiet room, which has a circle of chairs.
- ☀ Ground rules should be developed that foster a caring and warm atmosphere.
- ☀ The structured circle activities should address the needs of the children 'beyond'.
- ☀ Advocacy inside or outside the group is a guiding principle for all involved.

How does a Circle of Support differ from a class Circle Time?

Circle Time as part of the QCT model has been shown to help children develop their pro-social skills in a supportive and caring environment, in which everyone feels respected and valued. It provides opportunities for:

- ☀ listening;
- ☀ speaking;
- ☀ developing positive relationships;
- ☀ problem solving;
- ☀ empathy;
- ☀ enjoyment;
- ☀ celebration;
- ☀ peer support.

A Circle of Support also provides these opportunities, but within a smaller, more supportive and understanding context. It also offers the following:

- ☀ greater sense of pace;
- ☀ engaging and time-bound activities;
- ☀ more supervision;
- ☀ greater use of familiar rituals;
- ☀ occasionally, simplified versions of games and activities;
- ☀ greater opportunities for guaranteed success.

The three Rs – relationships, resilience and resourcefulness

Being shown how to develop relationships, resilience and resourcefulness may have a profound effect on children's self-esteem, and help them to manage their feelings effectively. Activities in a Circle of Support can be tailored to enable each child to achieve this. The presence of two adults means that the level of input and supervision is high. The activities are designed to be structured, lively and enjoyable, and to provide appropriate help for the children.

Within a Circle of Support, children 'beyond' are taught specific emotional literacy and social skills, and are provided with opportunities to build a positive self-image – their negative self-image is challenged by the activities, by themselves and by their peers.

THE PRESENCE OF TWO ADULTS MEANS THAT THE LEVEL OF INPUT IS HIGH.

Theoretical underpinnings of a Circle of Support

The Circle of Support model has arisen out of practical experience. However, as the following paragraphs show, a number of theories point to reasons why it has the potential to be successful.

Emotional literacy

Being emotionally literate is crucial for personal and academic success. For those children who struggle in this area there are huge repercussions. Their difficulties may affect their emotional security and relationships, which have a bearing on their future success. Some children need extra support to access the emotional curriculum that schools offer. For these children the classroom is too busy, crowded and distracting to take the opportunities offered to them. A well-supervised Circle of Support consisting of a carefully selected group of children engaged in differentiated activities makes emotional literacy more accessible to children 'beyond'.

FOR SOME CHILDREN THE CLASSROOM IS TOO DISTRACTING TO TAKE THE OPPORTUNITIES OFFERED TO THEM.

Behavioural approach

The underlying assumptions of this approach, based on the work of Pavlov and Skinner, are that emotional and behavioural problems are caused by aberrant learning. Advocates suggest that such problems can be resolved through 'unlearning' inappropriate behaviours and learning appropriate ones. The model relies upon positive reinforcement to strengthen appropriate behaviour (Cooper *et al.* 1994). A Circle of Support provides peer-led reinforcement and helps children to 'unlearn' inappropriate behaviours.

Person-centred therapy

The methodology for circles of support is influenced by humanistic psychology, particularly person-centred therapy developed by Carl Rogers (Rogers 1961 and 1970). Simply put, this theory suggests that we are able to grow emotionally only when we experience warmth, unconditional love and empathy. Rogers suggests that we grow through positive interactions with significant others in our lives.

Unfortunately, many children have not had stable, consistent and loving significant others, so they lack a frame of reference for their relationships and behaviours.

One of the key ideas of a Circle of Support is that it offers a child warmth and understanding that they can internalise. From this they can begin to form a different view of themselves. A small group that offers someone emotional and physical safety, warmth and a feeling of value can become a generalised other. This is a view expounded by G.H. Mead (1934). The generalised other may have a similar effect to that of a significant other in the emotional development and well-being of a person.

Cognitive-behavioural therapy

Some aspects of the cognitive-behavioural approach are reflected in a Circle of Support. The underlying assumption with this approach, as explored by many, including Donald Meichenbaum, is that cognitive processes can change behaviour, and so a child's perceptions are vital to understanding their behaviour (Meichenbaum 1977). Circles of support can help children to reassess their misconceptions and see themselves or their behaviour from another's perspective. Developing the ability to think empathetically is a key focus. This enables the child to challenge their preconceptions about themselves, broadening their view and prompting them to modify their behaviour as a result.

Social learning theory and reality therapy

The social learning model claims that a person's aspirations and self-concept influence their behaviour (Bandura 1977). They also learn through observing others. A Circle of Support facilitates such observational learning and the modelling that follows.

William Glasser developed reality therapy, based on the idea that all irresponsible or inappropriate behaviour is an unsuccessful attempt by a person to satisfy their need to love and be loved, and also their need to feel that they are worthwhile to themselves and others (Glasser 1965, 1975 and 1998). He noted that children who are taught social responsibility, how to help each other and how to solve problems are better able to cope with the problems of society. In reality therapy the facilitator and the group help the person they are working with to face their inappropriate behaviour, take responsibility for it and replace it with new and better ways of behaving. This is done within caring relationships and an accepting ethos.

Circle of friends intervention approach

A circle of friends, developed by Colin Newton and Derek Wilson, is a structured intervention based on the belief that a person's judgements about their behaviour and that of others can be influenced by the social situation. This intervention uses a structured circle approach to help a group to give a specific child positive attention (Taylor 1996 and 1997, and Newton and Wilson 1999). Activities undertaken are focused on increasing the child's self-esteem and the learning of new skills. This helps the child interpret and respond to their environment and social situations with understanding.

This method is a cost-intensive but effective way of tackling severe emotional and behavioural difficulties through the mobilisation of a person's peers. Circles of support offer the same positive attention in a similar atmosphere of warmth and encouragement, but include a wider group of 'needy' children and use a less structured approach.

The ecosystemic approach

Ecosystemic approaches to emotional and behavioural difficulties draw on an ecological perspective. They describe human behaviour in terms of finding and maintaining a balance that benefits people and their environments. This approach is based on the belief that a change in one part of a system will affect the whole system.

We believe that a Circle of Support is most successful when it is part of an ecosystemic approach embedded in a whole-school structure for emotional support. The QCT model is an example of an ecosystemic approach that supports all aspects of a child's school life by providing such things as safe boundaries, listening systems and incentives.

Action research involving circles of support – theory into practice

As well as demonstrating strong theoretical underpinnings, findings from research projects conducted by students on Jenny Mosley's MEd modules at Bristol University's School of Education indicate that circles of support are invaluable for pupils.

For example, a ten-week circle-of-support programme with eight 12-year-old children had a positive impact on their perception of their social acceptance. Such results after only a short programme indicate the impact a Circle of Support may have.

Short-term circle interventions may also help children to become more reflective and aware of their feelings.

Longer programmes are required in order to address deep-rooted problems. These require longer intervention before a measurable change in a child's behaviour is apparent. A child with more intractable problems will be likely to need more time in a Circle of Support. This is one of the key reasons for early intervention before problems become embedded.

Circles of support were used successfully in 2004 in the Compass for Life project in Stirling (**www.stirling.gov.uk**). Here, accredited QCT trainers worked with people aged between 14 and 25 years, using a multi-agency approach that focused on employability through participative learning programmes. All the young people involved in the project had encountered barriers to accessing mainstream training and employment.

Circles of support were used to help the participants become more self-aware, and to develop their thinking and understanding of the world. The overall response after a three-month programme was positive, the main points being that it:

- created a positive atmosphere;
- was enjoyable;
- helped them understand others better;
- stopped the use of put downs;
- helped them to appreciate what others had to say.

If you would like to learn more about the research that has been carried out in this area, do go to our website, **www.circle-time.co.uk**, where you will find a forum to discuss research opportunities and findings. More research is needed in this area.

Key points

★ A Circle of Support is an intervention for children with needs above and beyond Wave 1 of QCT.

★ A Circle of Support is a group of eight to twelve children, possibly of mixed ages, supported by two adult facilitators.

★ The children who attend a group should consist of four to six children 'beyond' and up to four other children who will benefit from working in a small group, but have good social and behavioural skills.

★ The activities require a circle of chairs and should take place in a location where the participants will not be disturbed. The activities are planned in advance.

★ Circles of support are underpinned by a wide range of research and theory.

★ Several small-scale research projects for secondary pupils have indicated the usefulness and effectiveness of this type of intervention.

5 Planning your Circle of Support

When to offer a child a place in a Circle of Support

We consider Wave-1 strategies to be crucial to the smooth running of a school and have provided further details of these in Appendix 1 (page 162). The majority of the class should respond well to such positive behavioural systems and peer-support strategies. With these in place any children 'beyond' should become apparent as, although they may respond to one or two of them, overall the systems are not effective for them. Their needs are not being met and they are unhappy and/or display challenging behaviour.

The checklist on page 42 will help you to assess if a potential child 'beyond' has received adequate Wave-1 support. If they have, but they are still not responding, they should move to Wave 2 and be offered a place in a Circle of Support. If you feel that some of your Wave-1 systems are not functioning sufficiently, we recommend you to refer to Appendix 1 for further guidance before moving on to Wave 2.

The importance of school backing

Once you have established that you have a child who would benefit from a Circle of Support, it is important that you have the school's backing. Discuss with your headteacher what you would like to do and make sure that everyone who works with the child understands what will happen. Ideally all involved would attend a meeting about your plans, but we realise that this may be difficult to achieve. It is, therefore, important to inform as many staff members as possible, especially those who have most contact time with the child, and to include their parents or carers.

Who makes up a Circle of Support?

The most effective circle is made up of the following:

* ※ two adult facilitators;
* ※ four to six children 'beyond';
* ※ up to four children who are not 'beyond' but will benefit from attending the circle, as well as being positive role models.

Children in the last category might include those who seek attention, those who are withdrawn, and children with good social skills who need some extra attention. Such children may be experiencing difficult circumstances. The support of a small group may help them with feelings of vulnerability. Every child who attends a Circle of Support should benefit from it.

We recommend up to ten children in a group, although you can go up to twelve. It's a good idea to have a mix of ages – you might do this by key stage.

How is a child referred to a Circle of Support?

Children will usually be referred to a Circle of Support by their teachers. We have seen the following other referral routes in schools:

* ※ staff meetings that focus on supporting children 'beyond' with all relevant adults attending, including midday supervisors;
* ※ attitudinal or behavioural questionnaires;
* ※ parent referral;
* ※ self-referral through discussion with a child using the Wave-1 listening systems of QCT.

It is important that the adults working with children 'beyond' liaise with one another. This avoids an inconsistent approach that will create more fragmentation for the child involved.

Who should facilitate a Circle of Support?

We recommend that there are two co-workers present. These could be from the following categories: teachers, TAs, the SENCo, learning mentors and behaviour support co-ordinators. We have met charity outreach workers and other project members operating small circles. We strongly recommend that at least one of the facilitators is in school for most of the week as this means that the child 'beyond' has someone to be their advocate if necessary. In Scotland we have seen some behaviour support teachers taking class circle times so that the teachers can run circles of support.

The SEAL resources state that an effective facilitator:

☀ is enthusiastic – has a positive approach to children and activities;
☀ maintains good eye contact and is able to be emotionally warm;
☀ has empathetic listening skills;
☀ is able to recap and confirm what a child has said;
☀ is able to plan and deliver lively, active sessions;
☀ is encouraging;
☀ responds proactively to negative behaviour;
☀ enables members of the circle to have fun;
☀ works well with the other facilitator.

How do the co-workers work together?

Having two adults leading a Circle of Support means that they can model how to act in the circle. Children 'beyond' can push you to your limits, and it is vital that when one adult needs a break from being relentlessly positive, the other can take over. You may like to agree on a sign as a clue to your co-worker that you need to distance yourself for a while. It is important that the facilitators decide in advance on the language they will use, the qualities they will praise, and how a session will be run.

Older children such as sixth-form students can be drafted into a primary-age Circle of Support to act as role models. This can be an enormous confidence booster for the sixth formers, as well as benefiting the younger children. We recommend the same approach to pupil referral units.

How are the children involved?

It is important that each child is interviewed so they know why they have been chosen to join a Circle of Support. Based on this information, they need to make a clear decision to join the group and to commit to working as part of it. Ideally a child would talk to you about the areas in which they need help. If this is not possible, a child will still benefit from being told why they have been referred. That may empower them and make them feel that they have chosen to attend the circle.

How to interview a child

Some facilitators prefer a general interview with a child, while others like to use a questionnaire that will help to bring out the key issues (see page 151). Whichever approach you choose, it is helpful to give a child an idea of for how long they may be attending the circle, even though this may need reviewing after some weeks. Below are some of the things you may like to say or ask during an interview:

- ※ We think you might like some support for . . .
- ※ Is there anything that you would like help with?
- ※ We think being in a smaller group will help you and that you will help some of the other group members.
- ※ You can choose if you would like to go to this new group.
- ※ Are there any questions that you would like to ask about this?
- ※ We shall be letting [child's primary carer(s)] know that we are offering you some extra help in a small group to . . .
- ※ What sorts of changes would you like to make about how you are in school?
- ※ I want to thank your teacher for suggesting that you come to the group. We're looking forward to having you.
- ※ If you tell us something that is really important in the circle, we may have to tell other people who care about you, but we will always let you know that we are going to do this. (Revisit this during the programme.)

We believe that you should not offer complete confidentiality. As most teachers are not trained therapists, we suggest that you say to children that if anything is said or done in the group that worries you, you may have to discuss this with other members of staff. If such a situation occurs, the child involved should be informed.

One of the aims of the interview process is to show the child that continuous support is available and that the adults involved care about them. We suggest that the facilitators meet at least every other week with the child, the child's teacher and other parties involved to see how things are going. This helps the child to realise that there are a number of people who care about them and want the best for them.

It can be easy for the child to see their teacher as the bad cop and the facilitators as the good cops. The idea of a continuum of care – where the teacher is acknowledged for bringing the child to the circle – helps avoid this situation. When the child realises that the teacher is the one caring enough to offer them the opportunity of joining the group, they will not have such a polarised view of the adults involved. It's essential that the child meets the teacher and facilitators regularly – they benefit from seeing the adults together in this supportive manner.

What do facilitators need most?

Time is often the greatest barrier to running a successful Circle of Support. Time is needed for speaking to the relevant staff, interviewing the children and planning the sessions – including the themes, activities and the facilitators' role. In an ideal world, the two facilitators should also be able to support the child's teacher in a non-judgemental way.

How long should a session last?

Generally we recommend that a group meets every week, that each session lasts up to forty-five minutes, and that it is conducted at a brisk pace. However, at the beginning shorter sessions may be more appropriate to help the children become used to the new routines.

Some schools run their circles of support at the same time as their circle times, ensuring the teacher can give their attention to the group without being distracted by the needs of a child 'beyond'. Others prefer to hold them at a different time so that the children can come to Circle Time as well as the Circle of Support. Some schools run their smaller circles at lunchtimes, although they risk the children involved thinking that they are being penalised.

How many sessions do children need?

A Circle of Support normally runs for at least a term, but it can go on for longer. You will need to assess progress as the term passes – children will need different lengths of intervention. When you do decide that a child is ready to return full-time to the classroom, one of the facilitators could attend the class Circle Time for several weeks, introducing games and activities that the child 'beyond' excels at. The child 'beyond' can also introduce new games that they have learnt. This will boost their popularity with their peers.

The venue

The room you use will need to be big enough for a circle of the right number of chairs. There needs to be space for activities inside the circle. Make sure you have a Do Not Disturb sign for the door.

Think through how you will get the children to the room. In what order will you collect them from their classrooms, and what route will you take back to the room so that they arrive calmly?

Informing parents or carers

When you are sure that a child will benefit from attending a Circle of Support, a letter should be sent out to inform the child's parents or carers of your plans before the sessions start. You could use a letter like the one on page 41.

Some schools provide support for parents of children 'beyond', often in conjunction with health visitors or social workers. Such opportunities are rare, but valuable. There often comes a stage in a Circle of Support when the facilitators feel happy to allow children to invite people to the sessions to work with them. Such people might include a parent or carer, teacher, assistant or friend.

Key points

★ A child 'beyond' will not be fully responsive to Wave-1 classroom-management systems.

★ Getting the school and all the adults involved to support your small-group work is fundamental to setting up your Circle of Support.

★ A Circle of Support consists of two facilitators, four to six children 'beyond' and a group of up to four other children. The children may be of different ages.

★ The additional children in the group need to have good social skills and be able to benefit in some way from attending.

★ At least one of the facilitators should be in school for most of the week and have a visible role.

★ The facilitators should interview each child before the group starts, to help manage their expectations and check that the child is in favour of joining.

★ It is important that the facilitators work with a child's teacher so that the teacher is seen to support the child's time in the group actively.

★ A Circle of Support usually runs once a week for a term. Each session is approximately forty-five minutes long, although the initial sessions may be shorter.

★ The venue should have room for a circle of chairs with space in the middle for activities.

Dear

We are pleased that your child has been making progress at school in

_____

However, to help their social progress, we feel they would benefit from more support with some specific social skills. We are running a special booster programme, approximately once a week for . . . minutes, during which we will be focusing on these skills. We would like to invite your child to participate in this group.

If you have any questions, please do contact me.

Yours sincerely

- -

Dear

We are pleased that your child has been making progress at school in

_____

However, to help their social progress, we feel they would benefit from more support with some specific social skills. We are running a special booster programme, approximately once a week for . . . minutes, during which we will be focusing on these skills. We would like to invite your child to participate in this group.

If you have any questions, please do contact me.

Yours sincerely

Is a child receiving adequate Wave-1 support?

These questions will help you to decide if your school is doing enough to support a child before recommending them for a Circle of Support.

	Yes	No	Action plan
Am I looking after myself so that I have the energy and patience for this child?			
Have I sought help and support for the child whom I'm concerned about?			
If I'm not getting support and help in school, do I know where I can go to get it?			
Has this child experienced regular, well-organised weekly circle times in the classroom?			
Have I offered the child Bubble Time?			
Has the child been offered a Think Time Book to record their feelings in? Do they know where to put it so that I can look at it and reply?			
Are the moral values, the Golden Rules, displayed inside and outside the school buildings?			
Has the child experienced a range of rewards, including certificates for small targets signed by their peers?			
Has the child been offered the regular reward of responsibilities that they can carry out successfully?			
Has the child experienced the sanction of the withdrawal of a self-chosen privilege? We call this system Golden Time.			
Has this child been involved in a lunchtime community taskforce to ensure they keep out of trouble?			

6 What happens in a Circle of Support?

In this chapter we address some of the practical issues involved in running a Circle of Support. We have worked with such therapeutic circles for many years and patterns of good practice have emerged. Supported by the theory we have explored in previous chapters, this information – derived from case studies – will help you to set up your own circle.

Planning your themes

The key to running a successful Circle of Support is careful planning. This begins with the facilitators consulting the people who work with the chosen children in order to learn about the children's needs. After this, you will need to decide whether to focus on a broad theme such as building self-esteem, or to choose a specific theme such as:

- ❋ anger management;
- ❋ trust;
- ❋ self-confidence;
- ❋ assertiveness;
- ❋ empathy.

You may decide to develop themes based on your school's PSHE curriculum or the SEAL resources.

Whatever you choose should be informed by your evaluation of the children's needs, based on your interview with each child and discussions with the adults who work with them. In Chapter 12 there is information on assessment that will help to inform your planning at this stage.

Circle of Support session plans

Each of the next two chapters includes a series of sessions for you to use. The first series is designed to help facilitators and children to become used to the group and the format. These sessions are shorter and more straightforward than the later ones. We have included work on the following five skills, with which children 'beyond' often struggle: looking, speaking, listening, thinking, and concentrating.

The themes for the second set of sessions are as follows:

- ☀ safety;
- ☀ emotions and how to manage them;
- ☀ social skills;
- ☀ motivation;
- ☀ self-esteem.

These themes often underlie many of the difficulties that children 'beyond' face. For example, if a child has poor social skills and lacks self-esteem, these will be intrinsic to most of the challenges that the child faces. Supporting the child in these areas will help them in others. We have included safety as children 'beyond' may be more vulnerable or at risk than other children as their sense of self-preservation and clarity of thinking are likely not to be developed sufficiently.

Using a circle of chairs or the floor

We suggest using a circle of chairs for some activities. However, some children find sitting on a chair difficult. They may lack the confidence to do this and may squirm about on their chair as a result. Such restlessness will not help them or other group members. If the circle includes such a child, it may be better to begin a new Circle of Support with floor-based activities.

Floor-based games

Using the floor for activities suggests to participants that what they are going to do will be relaxed and comfortable. Both structured games – like giant Snakes and Ladders – and imaginary ones can be played on the floor. A wider circle of chairs can be retained as a boundary to help the children feel safe during such activities.

Choose your floor-based games with care. Some children in your group with self-confidence problems or low resilience may not cope with being eliminated from a game. However, this can be a useful experience once a child is feeling more resilient. A few examples of activities we use follow, and more appear in Chapter 7.

Kim's Game

Place ten small items on a tray. Give the children a minute to study the items before covering them with a cloth. When the time is up, cover the tray and go round each child in the circle and ask them to tell you an object on the tray. Vary the items and where you begin in the circle for repeats of the game on other occasions.

Musical Statues

Children walk around the inside of the circle with some music playing. When the music is paused, they have to keep still. Anyone who moves is out and sits at the edge.

Sleeping Pirate

Choose a child to sit in the middle of the circle with a blindfold on. They are the pirate. Place a tambourine or bunch of keys in front of them. Choose a child to try to pick the keys up and return to their place without the pirate hearing them. If the pirate thinks they hear something, they point in the direction of the noise. If they point at the child stealing the keys, they swap places. If not, they can have another go.

Parachute games

There are lots of enjoyable circle games that can be played using a parachute. You could put a light ball or balloon in the middle; everyone pulls on their part of the parachute to keep it moving or bouncing. Alternatively, put several beanbags on the parachute; the children jerk it to try to make them jump off. You could do the same with some skipping ropes. The book *Making Waves*, listed in the books and resources section of Chapter 13, offers a large collection of parachute games.

Co-operative construction

Creating something may help children to come together. Try providing sheets of newspaper for them to make sculptures in small groups without using any adhesive. Large construction equipment such as giant Lego® is good too.

Body art

The children use large sheets of paper or strips of wallpaper to express themselves through large-scale artwork. They can draw round each other, or round their own hands or feet. They can try drawing with their feet or the hand they don't normally use.

Sensory circles

If children 'beyond' can recognise and develop their sensory awareness, this helps them to understand their feelings. Try asking them to use their sense of taste to identify small pieces of fruit. Use a blindfold. Make sure you have checked on any allergies before playing this game. Alternatively, put items such as pieces of pasta, some sand, cotton wool, a small cuddly toy or leaves secretly in individual bags. Blindfold a child and ask them to use their sense of touch to guess what the item is. You could test their sense of smell with things such as lemon juice, Marmite and lavender in little bottles. For hearing, pass a bunch of keys or a tambourine round the circle, trying not to make a sound. If the children hear a noise, they put their hand up.

Twister

This popular game helps break down barriers between children.

Karaoke

If you have a karaoke machine or a games console with singing games, you can ask the children to sing along in pairs or groups.

Large-scale toys

If you have large versions of games for the playground, such as Connect 4, these can be used within the circle, provided there is room for them.

Beetle

The aim is to draw a beetle as quickly as possible. Divide the children into groups. Give each group a 1–6 die, a pencil and a piece of paper. The first child in each group rolls the die and, depending on their score, draws a part of a beetle that has not been drawn already. Play then moves to the next child. The first group to complete their beetle wins. The numbers on the die relate to the following beetle parts:

1 – three spots on one side of its body;

2 – one of the two antennae;

3 – three of the six legs;

4 – one of the two eyes;

5 – the body;

6 – the head.

Using board games

Board games are great for children 'beyond'. They teach how and why it is important to take turns and follow rules. Throwing a die is exciting or disappointing, depending on the score, as is landing on a snake or a ladder. Learning how to manage such feelings is an important skill, as is coping with losing a game.

Structuring the session

Children 'beyond' need a session with a good pace, a sense of routine, rituals and enjoyment for them to engage with the activities. We have a five-step model that provides opportunities to meet up, engage in some activities and end with a closing ritual. The children could sit on the chairs for the first and last activities, even if only for a short time. This increases the ritual aspect and also helps them to get used to using chairs. Once the children are comfortable with the circle format, choose one or two of the steps to use initially. Leave step 3, which requires the most empathy, until everyone is ready. Never end a session with step 3 as you will leave children at their most vulnerable.

1   Meeting up – playing a game

Begin the session with a pacy game that helps the children to relax and enjoy being part of the group. This game can involve the children changing seats so that the group is mixed up, providing opportunities for new friendships. You could call out different criteria for swapping seats, such as all children with blue on, who like apples, and so on.

2   Warming up – breaking the silence

This opportunity for speaking and listening should be as straightforward as possible, reducing threat or embarrassment. Each child is given an opportunity to speak. This involves a round in which one of the facilitators introduces a sentence stem, such as 'My favourite animal is . . .'. The child on the facilitator's left repeats the stem, adding their favourite animal. This continues round the circle and is finished by the facilitator, who completes the stem too.

A speaking object such as a painted wooden egg is used to denote whose turn it is to speak. Whoever is holding it has the right to speak without interruption. They pass the object on once they have finished.

Holding the speaking object does not oblige anyone to speak; any child who does not want to do so may say 'Pass'. If too many children are saying 'Pass', you could tell the children the theme of the round the day or week before, so that they have time to think of a sentence. Very shy children can write their sentence on a piece of card prior to the circle meeting so they can read it aloud.

If you need to intervene, you must go to the child who is holding the speaking object, put your hand on theirs and politely say what you need to say.

3   Opening up – exploring issues

Now the children should be ready to tackle something more challenging. This step is an opportunity for important issues to be discussed and for help to be sought. This encourages children to develop a belief in their ability to make responsible choices and decisions. Problem-solving skills can be practised. Children should remember to raise their hands or make a thumbs-up gesture before speaking. They can be asked to practise specific skills such as listening or speaking in turn. Alternatively, a child could ask the group for help with a problem. The members can make suggestions by using a simple sentence stem such as 'Would it help if . . .?' Stories, role play, games, puppets and dressing-up can be used to explore problems, concerns, fears or hopes in a sensitive way.

4   Cheering up – celebrating the positive

This is an opportunity for children to give and receive praise for their social and emotional achievements. This helps them to feel more competent and positive.

5 Calming down – bridging

The bridging step helps the children to make a calm transition to their next activity. It may involve a calm game, a song or a guided visualisation. The children learn through this that they can have quiet times safely and calm down, even when they are in a group.

Mixing the steps

Following this model will bring the circle to a close calmly. If you are running a shorter session or introducing the model, you may want to concentrate on step 2. You could introduce it between two steps 1s, using a sentence stem such as one of these:

- ☼ One thing I enjoyed about today was . . .
- ☼ One game I would like to do next time is . . .
- ☼ One thing I would have changed is . . .

This leads children gently into the routine and helps build their confidence in a slower and more lasting way. It is beneficial for the children to get a positive feeling from a shorter session. The sessions provided in this book start with fewer steps and build up to the five-step model.

When starting your Circle of Support, try to begin your second session by repeating the final game of session 1. This pattern can be repeated in subsequent sessions. Encourage the children to take the games they learn back to their classroom to show their peers. Remind their teachers to ask for demonstrations.

Using names in a Circle of Support

In Circle Time we ask children not to mention the names of other children negatively when they are talking about a problem. If they need to talk about someone by name, they should be offered an opportunity to talk on a one-to-one basis with the teacher in what we call Bubble Time. Ideally, the facilitators should offer Bubble Time too. If this is not possible and the children are not allowed to mention names, this can create issues. If you can trust your group not to take things that have been said in the circle beyond it, you could allow names to be used. Fortunately, the main thing the children will take from a session is what they experience last. This is why sessions finish with an enjoyable game or celebration.

What happens after a Circle of Support?

We recommend that one facilitator is available to speak to any group members who need to air concerns, while those that don't are walked back to their classes by the other facilitator. Alternatively, the facilitators could make themselves available later in the week.

It is important to bring each child, their teacher and the facilitators together every two or three weeks. The child can be asked what they would still like to learn as part of the group. The teacher too can be asked to suggest one thing that they would like the group to help the child with – for example sitting still, listening well or playing calmly with other children. The teacher should be thanked by the facilitators for suggesting that the child joined the group.

The facilitators need time to reflect

If at all possible, it is important for the facilitators to have at least fifteen minutes to reflect together on the outcomes and successes of the session. For example, if a parachute game was used and one child became overexcited, they could decide not to use that game for a few sessions and then reintroduce it to see if the child has learnt greater self-control. Try to talk about which children responded to an activity, which didn't, and why.

Introducing ground rules

Don't introduce rules in the first session as this can make the circle boring. If the session is heavy going, the children are more likely to sabotage it. Keep the first couple of sessions exciting and pacy. Introduce rules in the third or fourth session, once the children have decided that it is in their interest to come to the group. At this point, ask the children what rules they want to have.

In our experience, when children suggest rules they fall into the following categories:

- ❋ physical safety (being gentle);
- ❋ emotional safety (being kind);
- ❋ respect for each other (listen well);
- ❋ concentrate on the task in hand (work hard);
- ❋ respect for the environment (look after things);
- ❋ respect for the truth (being honest).

As well as such moral values, you may want to agree some practical routines, such as punctuality, tidying the room, putting thumbs up, and so on.

Introducing rewards and sanctions

You will need to discuss with the children what should happen if someone breaks a rule. The children's suggestions are usually as follows:

- ❋ give a verbal warning;
- ❋ use a visual warning – show a warning card;
- ❋ impose time out of the main group, using a sand timer
  next to a chair outside the circle;
- ❋ lose the privilege of coming to the next session.

Ask the children what should happen if they keep the rules or earn a reward. Their suggestions usually include these:

- ❋ retain the privilege of coming to the group;
- ❋ verbal praise from another group member;
- ❋ verbal praise to their teacher and parent or carer;
- ❋ use of rewards such as stickers and certificates.

In addition, you may want to introduce special incentives such as a certificate that could be sent to a significant other in the life of the child (see page 53).

Preparing for your session

Make sure you are well prepared for a session. Knowing what the session will involve, having resources to hand, and agreeing on a consistent approach from the facilitators will help the children to relax, feel safe and engage with what is going on. These are key elements of the facilitators' role.

When planning your session, think about what will happen before and after activities; foreseeing any transition problems will help the group run smoothly.

How to end a series of circles of support

The way in which a series ends is very important. For many children the Circle of Support is a safe haven. Don't underestimate the sense of loss that they may feel. Try to make a bridge to take the child back to the classroom full-time without arousing fear and panic. If you decide that a child is to leave the group, it is best to talk to them on their own and agree on this together. Include in the child's final sessions some activities that focus on loss and letting go. Give them a card with a photo of the group on the front and a best wishes message inside. Provide details about how to contact you if the child really needs to.

If you can support the child during their class Circle Time that would be ideal.

A checklist to help you plan your Circle of Support appears on page 54.

Key points

★ One of the keys to a successful Circle of Support is careful planning, including which areas to focus on.

★ The preliminary sessions in Chapter 7 build up to using the full five-step model. Chapter 8 includes plans for thirty full sessions.

★ If children have difficulty sitting on chairs initially, begin with largely floor-based activities, starting and ending the sessions on chairs.

★ Use floor-based activities as a bridge to using the five-step model.

★ Sessions need to be structured to suit the group's needs, and they should be pacy, with plenty of ritual and enjoyment.

★ After the preliminary sessions, the children should be ready for the full five-step model.

★ Try to provide time for children to meet with a facilitator if they have a concern. The facilitators need time to meet too.

★ The Circle of Support will need to have rules, sanctions and rewards in place after a few weeks.

★ When a child leaves the circle, they may feel a sense of loss. They need to be carefully integrated back into the classroom full-time.

Congratulations!

We are delighted that _____

has been coming to our small-circle group

and is making progress with

_____

Keep up the good work!

Signed _____

Congratulations!

We are delighted that _____

has been coming to our small-circle group

and is making progress with

_____

Keep up the good work!

Signed _____

A checklist for facilitators running a Circle of Support programme

1	Have we spoken to key people in school and gained their support?	☐
2	Have we identified a group of children from different classes and with different behaviours to form the group?	☐
3	Do we have the time we need to plan, and to discuss our aims, the language we will use and how we will work together?	☐
4	Are we and some of the children in the group able to demonstrate the social and emotional skills being promoted?	☐
5	Do we have a signal to each other to use if we need a short 'break' while running a circle?	☐
6	Have we agreed on the length of a session?	☐
7	Is it possible for one or both of us to make ourselves available for a few minutes after a session or at another time to talk to any group members who would like such an opportunity?	☐
8	Have we agreed on the number of weeks a circle will last?	☐
9	Have we introduced ground rules, sanctions and incentives?	☐
10	Have we thought about how to end a series of circles of support safely?	☐

7 Plans for preliminary sessions to develop basic social skills

The plans in this chapter focus on getting children enthused about a Circle of Support and used to its format. The middle section of each session is usually floor based. The plans emphasise the five learning skills of looking, listening, speaking, thinking and concentrating – understanding and practising these will help the children inside and outside the circle.

The plans that follow will help the children to practise acceptable social behaviour, which many children 'beyond' will not have experienced before. These preliminary sessions give them the opportunity to practise ways of interacting that, in due course, they will need to be able to use in a range of situations. We have tried to include simple games that can be played without complicated equipment in the hope that the children will play them at home.

The ultimate aim of these preliminary sessions is to lead the children, gently and safely, to full participation in the five-step model for a Circle of Support. The length of time for each session increases as you work through them.

For all sessions, make sure you have read through the relevant plan carefully and prepared the room in advance. Agree what each facilitator is going to do, and whether they will be involved or acting as an observer.

Make a circle of chairs to act as a safe boundary for the floor-based activities.

Session 1

Resources

Construction kits and a bunch of keys

What to do

A. Begin by leading the group in a game that includes some simple warm-up exercises, such as rolling your shoulders, flexing your wrists, and wiggling your fingers. Switch is a good game for this. Start with one action, such as rolling your shoulders. Then change to another, such as flexing your wrists. At this point the children roll their shoulders. Each time you change, the children do the action before.

B. With the children sitting on the chairs, cheerfully introduce each child to the group. Add a chair to the circle on your right. Look at one of the children and say, 'Hello . . ., nice to meet you. Please join me.' This creates a spare chair elsewhere in the circle. The child who now has a space on their right asks a different child to join them. Continue until all the children have moved. At this stage if a child finds it difficult to speak, they can use gestures with an open hand.

C. Put out the construction sets on the floor and ask the children to make houses. Let them choose whether they wish to work alone, in pairs or in a small group. One facilitator could make notes about how they approach this task and the social interactions that take place.

D. Make a positive comment about each model. If a child destroys their work, don't make a fuss. Say calmly, 'Sometimes things you want to make don't turn out right. It can be annoying.'

E. Ask the group to stand in a tight circle while you stand in the middle. One child is given the keys and puts them behind their back. The group has to try to pass the keys from person to person without your guessing who has the keys at any given point. If you think you know who has the keys, point to that person. If they are holding the keys, you can stay in the middle and the game continues. If they are not holding the keys, you swap places with them and a new round begins.

This game is exciting, as well as enabling the children to be in close proximity with each other in a positive manner.

F. Ask the children to sit on the chairs. Use the keys for this game. The aim is to try to pass the keys round the circle without making a sound. At the end of the game, thank the children for their self-control and ability to create silence when it was needed.

Session 2

Resources

Construction kits and a tambourine

What to do

A. Repeat the final game of the previous session. Ask the children to sit on the chairs. Use the tambourine for this version of the game. The aim is to try to pass it round the circle without making a sound. This game will help the children to reconnect with the positive feelings they experienced before.

B. Tell the children that they need to work as a group to make an adventure playground, wildlife park or theme park using the construction materials. Alternatively, use a 5- or 10-minute sand timer and ask them to build the tallest tower they can before the time runs out; or tip the pieces on the floor and ask the children to sort them into categories within the time limit. Make sure you praise any co-operation.

C. Ask the group to stand in an inward-facing circle. When you say 'Left', the group must shuffle in a clockwise direction until everyone is roughly back where they started. Repeat this, but keep changing the direction you call.

D. Play the same game sitting on the chairs so that the children must move from seat to seat.

E. Repeat the first game of this session. Explain that having such a quiet room makes it easier to listen to each other. Give each child a sticker as a reward for good listening.

Session 3

Resources

Newspapers, sticky tape, scissors, an empty plastic bottle, and a tambourine

What to do

A. Begin with the tambourine game from the previous session. This time the children must try to pass it silently round the circle with their eyes shut.

B. Tell the group that you want them to work together to make the tallest free-standing newspaper tower that they can.

C. After the task, praise any pro-social behaviour. Ask the group to comment on any problems that arose and suggest solutions. For example, if sharing the tape was difficult, ask what ways there are in which it could have been used so that everyone could get a bit when they needed to. Use the sentence stem 'Would it help if . . .'.

D. For this game the children need to sit on the chairs. Explain that the bottle contains snake venom. It must be passed from person to person with great care. On subsequent rounds you can add further challenges, such as passing the bottle without using hands or with knees only, and as fast as possible.

E. Perform a round using the sentence stem 'The circle game I like best is . . .'.

Session 4

Resources

Five A5 cards numbered 4–8, eight non-slip circles and a box with a lid holding a number of familiar objects

What to do

A. Play a game from a previous session.

B. Describe a scenario that requires the group to move from one side of the circle to the other, such as crossing a river, boggy ground or a lava field.

C. Ask the children to stand on one side of the circle. Choose one child to pick a card with their eyes closed. The number on the card shows how many cardboard circles the group may use.

D. Explain that the group must move from one side of the circle to the other using the non-slip circles as stepping stones. They can't touch the floor at all.

E. If there is time, you can play this again, perhaps with a time limit.

F. Finish with a round using the chairs and the sentence stem 'One person I'd like to thank for helping me is . . .'.

Session 5

Resources

A large piece of paper, three different-coloured marker pens, sheets of A4 paper, different-coloured felt pens and a beanbag

What to do

A. Play a game from a previous session.

B. Put the large piece of paper on the floor and use a marker pen to draw four rows of four dots on it.

C. Divide the group into two teams (A and B). Give each team a marker pen. Ask them to take turns to join two dots with a line. The aim is to complete a square or rectangle by drawing the fourth line. When a team completes a square or rectangle, they write their team letter in it. When all the shapes are completed, the game is over and the team with the most is the winner.

D. Discuss how it feels to win and lose. Talk about strategies for coping with disappointment and how to be a sensitive winner.

E. Repeat the game in pairs using the A4 paper and felt pens.

F. Ask the children to sit on the chairs for a game called Meteorite. Explain that the beanbag is a very hot meteorite that must be passed round the circle as quickly and safely as possible.

G. On subsequent rounds you can add further challenges, such as using no hands or with elbows only.

H. End with a round using the sentence 'I hardly ever win at . . . but I enjoy playing it.'

Session 6

Resources

One large piece of paper, one marker pen, and a beanbag for every child

What to do

A. Play a game from a previous session.

B. Ask the children to remain on the chairs. Put the paper on the floor and divide it into five sections with the pen. Write a different instruction in each section, such as 'Stand up', 'Turn round', 'Hop', 'Sit on the floor', 'Kneel on the floor'. Use simple drawings instead if you have children with reading difficulties.

C. Each child takes a turn to throw their beanbag onto the paper. The group must follow the instruction it lands on.

D. Turn the paper over, divide it up as before, and ask the group to suggest some new workable commands. Write these on the paper and resume the game.

E. Play a game of beanbag statues. Each child puts a beanbag on their head and walks around inside the circle. They must not touch their beanbag with their hands. If their beanbag falls off, they must stand still until another child picks it up and puts it back. If the second child's beanbag falls off in the process, they must stand still too.

F. With the children sitting on the chairs, conduct a round using the sentence stem 'In today's circle I enjoyed . . .'.

Session 7

Resources

A large plastic bottle, a large ball, and a collection of smaller balls

What to do

A. Play a game from a previous session.

B. Tell the group that they must remain in their seats for the next game. Put the empty bottle in the centre of the circle. You can put some water or sand in the bottle and screw the lid on to keep it stable.

C. Roll the large ball as near to the bottle as possible.

D. Give each child at least one small ball. Ask them in turn to roll their ball to try to move the larger ball closer to the bottle. When someone manages to knock the bottle over, give them a clap. Play this a few times.

E. Stand in the middle of the circle. Walk towards one of the group, crouch down to their eye level and say warmly, 'If you know my name, please smile.' The seated child replies, 'I know your name, it is . . ., but I'm not going to smile.' You then try to make the person smile by telling a joke or making a funny face. If they manage not to smile, you move on to someone else. If they do smile they swap with you and the game continues.

F. End with a round using the stem 'One thing that makes me smile is. . .'. Gradually you are getting the children to talk about their feelings in safe ways.

Session 8

Resources

A large shirt

What to do

A. Play a game from a previous session in which the children swap places.

B. Ask for two volunteers to stand in the middle of the circle. Put the shirt on one of them and button it up. Tell the two children to hold hands.

C. Then ask for another volunteer to move the shirt carefully from one person to the other – it will be inside out when they have finished. Repeat with other children.

D. Ask the children to talk about how they felt in the different roles. Were they happy, puzzled or frustrated? Talk about how people may feel differently in the same situation – some people like to receive a prize during an assembly, while others would feel embarrassed. Discuss how we know what we are feeling. This can open up some helpful discussion on self-awareness.

E. Ask everyone to sit on the chairs for a round using the stem 'I thought the shirt game was . . .'.

Session 9

Resources

A large picture cut into the same number of pieces as there are members in the group

What to do

A. Ask the children to sit on the floor with a partner. Explain that you will call instructions that they need to respond to, either sitting or standing. For example, if you call 'One elbow to one knee', they must respond by standing or sitting with these body parts touching.

B. Sit on the chairs and send a movement round the circle. If you call 'Chin to knee', the person on your right touches their chin to the knee of the person on their right. This continues round the circle.

C. Give out the cut-up pieces of the picture. Ask for two volunteers to organise its completion.

D. Watch how they manage this task and make positive comments on what they did well. Play the game a couple more times.

 Ask the children to sit back on their chairs and play the smile game as follows. Stand in the middle of the circle. Walk towards one of the group, crouch down to their eye level and say warmly, 'If you know my name, please smile.' The seated child replies, 'I know your name, it is . . ., but I'm not going to smile.' You then try to make the person smile by telling a joke or making a funny face. If they manage not to smile, you move on to someone else. If they do smile they swap with you and the game continues.

E. Give a sticker that says 'Thank you for being helpful' to any of the children whom you saw co-operating effectively.

Session 10

Resources

A number of small items in a bag, a sheet of thick card and a selection of small balls

What to do

A. Give the bag to the child on the chair to your right. The bag continues round the group until you finish the following chant:

> *Diggery doo, diggery doo,*
> *What am I*
> *Going to do*
> *With this diggery, diggery,*
> *Diggery doo?* (Clap)

B. When you clap, the child holding the bag takes out an item and tells the group about it – what it is called, what it does, whether or not they like it, and so on.

C. Play a balancing game. Two volunteers go to the centre of the circle and hold one end of the card each. Place one or more of the balls on the card. Ask the volunteers to walk round the circle keeping the balls on the card.

D. Ask the other children to suggest ways in which the volunteers could move. The volunteers should try these, but if they feel a command is unreasonable, they can offer the card to the person who gave the command, saying 'That's too much for me. You said it so you can do it!' Then the child who gave the command must choose a partner and the two swap places with the children holding the card.

E. Sitting in the chairs, ask the children to complete the round 'I thought the game was fair/unfair because . . .'. Thank the children for their thoughts.

Building up to using the five steps

These transitional sessions will help facilitators and children to get used to the five-step model. Begin each session with a game from an earlier circle that the group enjoyed.

Session 1

A. Ask each child to complete the following sentence using the speaking object: 'I feel happy when . . .'.

B. Ask everyone in the circle to join hands, to breathe in as you count to 3 and to breathe out to the same count. Pick a child, tell everyone else to close their eyes, and ask the chosen child to squeeze gently the hand of the child on their left, who then does the same to the child on their left and so on round the circle.

Session 2

A. Ask each child to complete the following sentence using the speaking object: 'If I had a million pounds, I would . . .'.

B. Ask the children to nominate someone who has done well in a specific area that week, such as remaining calm. If most of the children agree with a nomination, they all sign a certificate. Present this to the nominated child, saying, 'Well done, [name], you've . . . all week.'

Session 3

A. Ask each child to complete the following sentence using the speaking object:

'If I were an animal, I would be . . .'.

B. Ask the children to stand up and chant 'We are special.' Each time they say 'special' they raise their arms above their heads.

C. Ask the children to sit on their chairs with their hands in their laps and their backs straight. Ask them to close their eyes and think about their breathing. Tell them that as they breathe in you want them to breathe in a feeling of happiness, and as they breathe out you want them to breathe out anything that may be making them unhappy. Allow a minute or so for this. Now, ask them to imagine a screen on which they can see themselves spending a warm summer's day doing something they really enjoy. Ask them to experience this picture and to open their eyes when they are ready.

Session 4

A. Ask each child to complete the following sentence using the speaking object: 'At school, I like . . .'.

B. Explore the children's talents for movement. Ask volunteers to show a gym or dance move they know. Tell them to introduce it with the sentence stem 'My name is . . . and I can . . .'. Encourage them to talk about the difficulties they experienced as they learnt the movement and how they felt when they had mastered it.

C. Finish with a game the group enjoyed from an earlier session.

Session 5

A. Ask each child to complete the following sentence using the speaking object: 'My favourite lunch is . . .'.

B. Read a short story to the group, such as a fairy story. Pretend to be one of the characters and ask the group to interview you. This is called 'hotseating'. Encourage the group to ask questions such as these:

- ☀ What did you think when . . . happened?
- ☀ How did it make you feel?
- ☀ Why did you act in the way that you did?

C. Ask the children to stand up and chant 'We are special.' Each time they say 'special' they raise their arms above their heads.

8 Five-step session plans

The thirty sessions that follow are designed to cover some of the key themes for children 'beyond'. If your group is ready, you can use them as they are or adapt them to suit your needs. The sessions are organised into five sets of six meetings, each set exploring a particular theme.

The skills and attitudes that are investigated in step 3 of each session will need to be revisited if they are to be securely accessed by the more vulnerable members of your group. For this reason, we have provided some extension activities, and we advise you to repeat sessions as often as necessary.

Keep resources for some floor-based activities in the room in case a session is not going well. Have a small stock of music CDs to hand for background music – choose music that will soothe, calm and relax.

Safety

1 *We understand the meaning of danger*

Key word

Danger: something that may cause harm, injury or loss

Resources

A flipchart and a pen

Meeting up

Ask the children to sit in a space on the floor and demonstrate the following actions:

- ☀ row the boat – sit on the floor and mime rowing;
- ☀ man overboard – lie on your stomach and mime swimming;
- ☀ catch a fish – pretend to pull in a fish caught by a fishing rod;
- ☀ fish in the boat – lie on your back and wriggle;
- ☀ storm alert – sit with your head in your hands and shiver;
- ☀ all safe – lie on your back in a relaxed manner.

Briskly call out instructions to which the children have to respond quickly.

Warming up

Ask each child to complete the following sentence using a speaking object:
'I feel excited when . . .'.

Opening up

Talk about how frightening a storm at sea must be and how sailors may feel during one. Write their suggestions on the flipchart under the heading of 'Danger'. Remind the children that the opposite of danger is safety. Write this on the flipchart and write down the children's suggestions for how sailors might feel after a storm has passed. Comment that for people to experience the positive feelings on the flipchart, they need to feel safe.

Cheering up

Ask one of the children to go into the middle of the circle and nominate other members for a round of applause. Ask them to explain why they chose those children.

Calming down

Tell the children that they can calm themselves when they are distressed by concentrating on their breathing. Demonstrate sitting still and breathing steadily and regularly. Ask the children to try it for a few minutes.

Extension activities

Give the children different dangerous scenarios, such as being chased by a wild animal, and alien attack. Ask them to act out two short scenes, one that shows how the danger felt and the other that shows how welcome a safe resolution is.

You might want to use a technique called 'thought tapping' during the scenes. The scene is paused by using the word 'Freeze'. Each character is then asked to tell the group their thoughts and feelings.

2 *We understand that safety is important*

Key word
Safe: not in danger – in a situation that offers protection, making harm unlikely

Resources
A bag containing a coin, a pencil, a key, a milk carton, a mobile phone and a picture of a pet

Meeting up
Ask the children to sit in a space on the floor and demonstrate the following actions:

- ☀ fit your skis – stand still and stamp your feet on the floor;
- ☀ ski downhill – bend your knees and stand in a tuck position;
- ☀ throw a snowball – pretend to make a snowball and throw it in the air;
- ☀ ski jump – stand with straight legs with your arms by your side and lean forward;
- ☀ snow storm – walk in slow motion against a strong wind;
- ☀ sun lounger – lie on your back in a relaxed manner.

Briskly call out instructions to which the children have to respond quickly.

Warming up
Ask each child to complete the following sentence using a speaking object: 'I feel safe when . . .'.

Opening up
Recap on the work done on danger and safety. Give the bag containing the items to one child and ask them to take one thing out and talk about how to keep it safe. Help by repeating the dangers that they mention, such as 'Yes, that's right, if you don't keep the coin somewhere safe you might lose it.' The bag is then passed to the next child. Sum up the various meanings of safety: protection from harm, loss, damage or tampering.

Introduce the idea that safety often involves something that we do. We can be safe by being in a certain place or with certain people, or by removing ourselves from a situation. Ask each member of the group to contribute one way in which they keep themselves safe.

Cheering up

Congratulate children by name for their suggestions. Explain that thinking skills are important and that by their contributions they have shown the ability to think carefully. Be specific in your praise, such as 'When you said that we need to keep dry to avoid getting a cold, you showed that you know something useful about how to stay healthy. Well done.'

Calming down

Ask everyone in the circle to join hands, to breathe in as you count to 3 and to breathe out to the same count. Pick a child, tell everyone else to close their eyes, and ask the chosen child to squeeze gently the hand of the child on their left, who then does the same to the child on their left and so on round the circle.

Extension activity

Show the children the things you usually bring to work. Point out that some of the items keep you safe: a coat in case it is cold or rains, a bag to stop you losing personal items, shoes to keep your feet dry. Explain that keeping ourselves and our possessions safe is something that happens all the time.

3 *We understand why we need rules (1)*

Key word

Rule: a guideline for action or behaviour

Resources

A flipchart, a pen, counters in two different colours, a bag and two balls of different sizes

Meeting up

Put the bag, counters and balls in the centre of the circle, choose two children and tell them to show the group how to play the game. When they look puzzled, ask them what's stopping them from playing. They are likely to say that you haven't told them the rules. Apologise and explain how to play:

- ※ Tell them which colour they need.
- ※ Put the counters in the bag.
- ※ Take a counter out without looking.
- ※ If the counter is the right colour, they bounce the larger ball for a minute.
- ※ If the counter is the other colour, they play catch with the smaller ball for a minute.
- ※ The other child then has a turn.

Allow them to play the game.

Warming up

Ask each child to complete the following sentence using the speaking object: 'My favourite game is . . .'.

Opening up

Point out that when we play a game, we need a set of rules. Rules guide us and show us what to do. Ask the group what games they enjoy. Choose one and write its rules on the flipchart. Write 'Rules help us to play together' underneath.

Cheering up

Congratulate the children on their interesting contributions and tell them that they are very good at noticing things and at sharing what they have learnt. Give each other a clap.

Calming down

Ask the children to sit on their chairs with their hands in their laps and straight backs. Ask them to close their eyes and think about their breathing. Tell them that as they breathe in, you want them to breathe in a feeling of happiness; and as they breathe out, you want them to breathe out anything that may be making them unhappy. Allow a minute or so for this. Now, ask them to imagine that they are looking through a window. They can see a lovely sandy beach. They open a door and go out to enjoy the fresh sea air and the sand between their toes. Ask them to enjoy this picture and to open their eyes when they are ready.

Extension activity

Ask children to bring their favourite board or playground game to a session and teach the others how to play it.

4 *We understand why we need rules (2)*

Key word
Rule: a guideline for action or behaviour

Resources
Two pieces of string or a piece of chalk

Meeting up
Ask the group to raise their arms as if holding the handlebars of a motorbike. Tell them to move around in this manner without touching one another. When they hear the following commands they must react quickly:

- ☼ Start the engine – lift right leg and pretend to kickstart the bike.
- ☼ Right turn – lean to the right.
- ☼ Left turn – lean to the left.
- ☼ Bumpy road – jump.
- ☼ Traffic lights – slow down and sit on the floor.

Warming up
Ask each child in turn to complete the following sentence using the speaking object: 'I like it when . . .'.

Opening up
Mark two lines about 1 metre apart on the floor using the string or chalk. Tell the children that what you have made represents a road. Line the children up on one side of the road. Tell them to cross the road one at a time. If a child uses the safe rules for crossing a road, they can stay on the other side. If they don't, you must call them back.

When a child makes it safely across the road, ask them to demonstrate how they did it – standing at the kerb, looking and listening, crossing sensibly, staying alert and continuing to look both ways. Point out that these rules help to protect us as we work and play together. Reiterate that safety is important, which is why we have rules.

Cheering up

Ask one of the children to go into the middle of the circle and nominate other members for a round of applause. Ask them to explain why they chose those children.

Calming down

Mime falling rain by waving your fingers. Send this mime round the circle. Now send thunder round the circle by slapping your thighs with your hands. Finally, mime the sun coming out by raising your arms above your head and then folding them in front of you. Send this action round the circle.

Extension activity

Ask the children to tell you other situations in which rules keep us safe, such as at the swimming pool, the railway station or in a car.

Put the children in pairs and give each pair a large sheet of paper and two pens. Ask them to draw a scene including safe and dangerous situations. Use the pictures to generate a list of rules to ensure that everyone in the scene stays safe.

5 *We know that groups need rules*

Key words

Ground rules: a set of agreed standards that allow meaningful dialogue while minimising conflict

Resources

A flipchart and a pen

Meeting up

Play the game of Captain's Coming using the following commands:

- ☀ on deck – sit in a circle;
- ☀ raise anchor – pretend to pull in a heavy anchor;
- ☀ captain's coming – stand to attention and salute;
- ☀ swab the deck – pretend to clean the deck with a mop;
- ☀ crow's nest – pretend to look through a telescope;
- ☀ galley – sit cross-legged on the floor.

Warming up

Ask each child to complete the following sentence using the speaking object: 'One rule that I know is . . .'.

Opening up

Recap on the usefulness of rules. Ask the children to think of ways to ensure that everyone involved in the circle enjoys themselves. Use their suggestions as a basis for the group's ground rules. Help the children to agree to rules that are appropriate to their needs. You will probably need to include such rules as these:

- ☀ We don't interrupt.
- ☀ We listen carefully.
- ☀ We don't use put downs.
- ☀ We are kind and helpful.
- ☀ We take turns.
- ☀ We work as a team.
- ☀ We think about problems and try to find solutions.

Write your ground rules on the flipchart.

Cheering up

Select a child who needs particular support or encouragement, and tell the group about something that they have done well recently. Say how pleasing this is and ask everyone to give them a round of applause. Ask the children if anyone has done something to make them happy that they would like to share. Praise their contributions.

Calming down

Ask the children to sit on their chairs with their hands in their laps and straight backs. Ask them to close their eyes and think about their breathing. Tell them that as they breathe in, you want them to breathe in a feeling of happiness; and as they breathe out, you want them to breathe out anything that may be making them unhappy. Allow a minute or so for this. Now, ask them to imagine that they are looking through a window. They can see a meadow filled with wild flowers. They open a door and go out to enjoy the smell of the flowers. Ask them to enjoy this picture and to open their eyes when they are ready.

Extension activities

Give out large sheets of paper and ask pairs or small groups to design posters to illustrate each of the ground rules.

Hold separate short sessions to clarify the meaning of each rule. For example, the children could research put downs by spending some time talking to each other about their experiences. Tasks like this will help to raise the self-esteem of group members.

Alternatively, do a survey about the number of times it is necessary to queue and take turns in a school day. The children could ask members of staff to talk about times when they queue and take turns outside school. This helps to show that ground rules are not restricted to school.

Ask the group to discuss the reasons for your school's rules. If children understand that the rules are for their benefit and safety, they are more likely to keep them.

6 *We agree to keep the group's rules*

Key word
Ground rules: a set of agreed standards that allow meaningful dialogue while minimising conflict

Resources
A list of the group's ground rules

Meeting up
Play Simon Says. You can take the role of leader yourself or choose a child to be leader. If an instruction is given with the prefix 'Simon says', the group must copy the leader's actions. If an instruction is given without the prefix, the group must not copy the leader's action. If they do, they must sit out for three instructions.

Warming up
Ask each child to complete the following sentence using the speaking object: 'I like it when we play . . .'.

Opening up
Look at the list of ground rules from the last session. Take each rule and ask the children to devise and act out scenes in which the rule is being broken. They can work in small groups. At the end of each scene, ask the group if they understand why the rule is important and why they should agree to try to keep it. If they are not convinced, listen to their objections and take a vote on whether to keep the rule or not.

Once you have an agreed set of rules, ask each of the children to sign the bottom of the list to show that they have made a contract to keep the ground rules.

Cheering up
Select two children whom you saw working well. Praise their co-operation skills. Ask everyone to give them a round of applause. Ask the two children whom they had noticed sharing well. Praise their contributions.

Calming down

Ask everyone in the circle to hold hands with the person on either side of them. Choose a child to begin by gently shaking the hand of the child on their left. They then shake the hand of the child on their left and so on until the round is completed.

Extension activity

Devise an activity that explores how treaties keep people safe and maintain the peace. You could focus on a historical event, a science-fiction film or an adventure story to show how kings and queens, starship captains and generals all sign treaties. You could draw up the treaty that might have been used in one of these scenarios.

Emotions and how to manage them

7 *We know that emotions involve feelings (1)*

Key word

Emotion: a feeling and its related psychological and biological states that make someone likely to act in a particular manner

Resources

A flipchart, a pen, pictures from magazines cut out and mounted on card; these need to depict people doing something.

Meeting up

Show the children a selection of actions that correspond with visual cues. For instance:

* ☀ when you clap your hands, they stand up and wave their arms;
* ☀ when you touch your head, they hop;
* ☀ when you tap your knees, they sit down;
* ☀ when you touch your nose, they clap their hands.

Play a game using these actions.

Warming up

Ask each child to complete the following sentence using the speaking object: 'I feel relaxed when . . .'.

Opening up

Recap on the ground rules contract in the previous session. Point out that the warming-up activity for this session involved looking and doing, and ask if they enjoyed the game. Use their responses to introduce the idea that feelings were involved.

Hold up one of the pictures and talk about what the people are doing. Repeat the children's ideas or write them on the flipchart. Ask if anyone can guess what the people might be thinking. This can be done by suggesting what the people might say. For example, a celebrating footballer might say, 'Wow, I scored a penalty!' Ask how the person might be feeling.

Point out that these three things – thinking, feeling and doing – are connected, and that the feeling or emotion often comes first.

Cheering up

Ask the children to stand up and chant 'We are important.' Each time they say 'important' they clap their hands above their heads.

Calming down

Ask the children to sit down, close their eyes and put their hands on their knees with the palms facing upwards and their fingers lightly curled. Most children find this comfortable as it relaxes their shoulders. Use a rainstick or some gentle music to create a calm background for the children to think about what makes them special.

Extension activities

Put the children in pairs and ask them in turn to tell each other something that happened recently at school, at home or elsewhere. Encourage the child who is listening to ask three questions:

※ What did you think when it happened?
※ How did you feel?
※ What did you do?

Read the children a short story and use the hotseating technique described on page 66 to ask one of the characters the three questions from the previous paragraph, and also to ask which reaction came first. You could go in the hotseat first before asking confident volunteers to have a turn. You could use the same technique for appropriate current events.

8 *We know that emotions involve feelings (2)*

Key word
Emotion: a feeling and its related psychological and biological states that make someone likely to act in a particular manner

Resources
A similar selection of pictures to those for the previous session, a rainstick or a recording of calm music

Meeting up
Call out different categories, such as anyone with a birthday in November, anyone who likes maths, anyone who enjoys swimming. A child who fits the category must walk to the centre of the circle and greet the other children there before sitting on a different seat.

Warming up
Ask each child to complete the following sentence using the speaking object: 'I feel enthusiastic when . . .'.

Opening up
Put the children in pairs and give them a picture. Ask them to discuss what emotions, thoughts and actions may be involved in the picture. Ask volunteers to show their picture and share their thinking about the thoughts, feelings and likely actions of the people in their picture. If some children give inappropriate responses, it probably means that the subject of emotion embarrasses them. Make a mental note of this and ask the rest of the group to help.

Use facial expressions to demonstrate a range of emotions. Ask the children to suggest emotions and demonstrate how these may look facially.

Cheering up
Select a child who would benefit from some encouragement, and tell the group about something that they have done well recently. Ask everyone to give them a round of applause.

Calming down

Ask the children to sit down, close their eyes and put their hands on their knees with the palms facing upwards and their fingers lightly curled. Most children find this comfortable as it relaxes their shoulders. Use a rainstick or some gentle music to create a calm background for the children to think about something that they have done well recently.

Extension activities

Ask the children to draw a picture of a person doing something exciting – such as skiing, hang-gliding or winning a competition – in the middle of a piece of paper. They should add a big thought bubble and fill it with the person's emotions and thoughts.

Draw short cartoon strips that show an exciting event happening in words and pictures.

9 *We know how to calm down*

Key words

Emotion, calm

Resources

A flipchart and a pen

Meeting up

Explain that you are all going to clap a pattern of four claps, after which you will call out instructions that the children must follow. For example:

clap four times;

clap high (*clap above your head*), 1, 2, 3, 4;

clap low (*clap by your knees*), 1, 2, 3, 4;

clap to the right, 1, 2, 3, 4;

clap to the left, 1, 2, 3, 4;

clap with a partner (*both hands together*), 1, 2, 3, 4.

Warming up

Ask each child to complete the following sentence using the speaking object: 'I feel peaceful when . . .'.

Opening up

Make a list together on the flipchart of all the words that mean 'angry' or 'annoyed'. Encourage the group to share the things they do to keep calm when life is stressful, or when they feel themselves becoming angry. Ask them to demonstrate these strategies so that other children can try them. Make a list of these on the flipchart. You might write such things as:

❋ breathe deeply;

❋ repeat a calming mantra like: 'cool, blue ocean';

❋ count slowly to 10 or backwards from 100;

❋ walk away from the problem;

❋ find somewhere quiet to calm down;

❋ talk to a safe adult;

❋ go somewhere and give a loud shout;

❋ find a soft object like a cushion to hit.

Put the children into small groups. Ask them to choose a calming technique and make up a short scenario to show how it might work in practice. First they need to think of a situation in which someone might get agitated, and then they should show how the technique helps prevent them from getting out of control. They could choose a group member to be a calming fairy or wizard who leaps in to save the situation by reminding the angry person of a suitable calming technique. Choose confident groups to show their plays to the rest of the group.

Ask each child which technique from the list they might try to use.

Cheering up
Ask one of the children to go into the middle of the circle and nominate other members for a cheer. Ask them to explain why they chose those children.

Calming down
Ask everyone to stand in a circle. Choose a child to begin by turning and bowing to the child on their left. They then bow to the child on their left and so on until the round is completed.

Extension activities
Make a group list on the flipchart of the times when it would be a good idea to use a calming technique. Ask them to describe or re-enact such situations and practise the calming technique they mentioned.

Ask each child to draw a picture of someone who needs to calm down. Give it a title such as 'Mrs More needs to calm down' and write what she should do underneath. Use these posters around the school so that the group can see that they have useful advice to share with the school.

10 *We can give and receive praise*

Key words
Praise, compliment

Resources
Examples of positive reinforcers used in your school, such as certificates and stickers, a flipchart, a pen

Meeting up
Exchange a high five with the child on your right, who then repeats this with the person on their right. This continues until the greeting has travelled round the circle.

Warming up
Ask each child to complete the following sentence using the speaking object: 'I like it when someone says . . .'.

Opening up
Talk with the children about the ways in which your school commends good work and behaviour. Show them examples of your school's rewards and talk about the pleasure adults in the school get from distributing them.

Talk about another good way to reward each other. It is easy and free and can make a difference to how we feel. It is often called 'praise' but can be called a compliment, a tribute, a commendation or congratulations. List these words on the flipchart and give some verbal examples, such as 'Well done', 'That's good.'

Model how to receive praise so that the giver knows they have been heard. Mention the following:

⁕ make eye contact;   ⁕ say 'Thank you' in a friendly voice.

This will help the children to avoid the following behaviours:

⁕ ignoring the praise giver;   ⁕ looking away;
⁕ frowning;   ⁕ mumbling.

Point out that as we give and receive praise, we should:

⁕ make eye contact;   ⁕ if giving praise, say clearly and
⁕ smile;   precisely what you are praising
⁕ speak in a friendly voice;   someone for.

Give the children opportunities to practise these skills by making up some appropriate scenarios, such as getting a spelling right – 'Well done, Martin. You have got the "e" and the "a" in the right order, which means that you have spelt "bear" and "fear" correctly.'

Put the children into pairs and ask them to think up a scenario in which each can praise the other.

Ask each child to make a list of situations outside school where they might give or receive praise.

Cheering up

Select two or three children and praise them for their input in the session. Comment on how they received the praise.

Calming down

Give the child on your right a thumbs-up sign. They repeat this action to the person on their right. This continues until the sign has travelled round the circle.

Extension activities

Encourage the group to share how praise makes them feel. Describe some appropriate scenarios and use them to explore the following questions:

- ※ What did you think when you were praised?
- ※ What did you do when you were praised?
- ※ How did you feel?

Many children with low self-esteem find receiving praise very difficult and tend to attribute praise and criticism to factors outside themselves. They have an external locus of control, which means that when they do something well they respond by thinking and saying such things as 'The teacher helped me' and 'I was lucky', rather than thinking 'I did well and earned this praise.'

Devise role-play opportunities to help the children understand that they can accept praise as something they can own. For instance, ask a child to act out being chosen to play the lead role in a film, and encourage them to make self-affirming statements such as 'I was chosen because I am a very talented actor.'

11 *We understand that we have responsibilities*

Key word
Responsibility: the state or position of being accountable to somebody or something

Resources
A selection of classroom equipment in a bag, paper and pencils

Meeting up
Choose one child to stand blindfolded in the centre of the circle. Pass an object such as a ruler or book round the circle until the child in the centre calls 'Stop'. Choose a child or pair of children to give the child verbal directions to locate the object. When the object has been found, choose another child to be blindfolded.

Warming up
Ask each child to complete the following sentence using the speaking object: 'I feel unhappy when . . .'.

Opening up
Hold up one of the objects from the bag, such as a pack of felt pens, and ask the children what needs to be done to keep it usable. Make a list of the group's suggestions. Discuss who is responsible for each item on the list; for example:

* ❊ each child is responsible for putting the tops back on the pens so they don't dry up;
* ❊ the teacher is responsible for making sure that there are enough felt pens;
* ❊ the monitors are responsible for making sure the pens are put away at the end of an activity.

Use the word 'responsible' frequently and explain its meaning.

Put the children in pairs and give each one a piece of classroom equipment. Ask them to make a short list of ways in which it should be cared for, and of who is responsible for each one. Ask confident pairs to share their thoughts.

Ask the children to discuss what their responsibility may be in such a situation as the following:

☀ One of your friends is unkind to you and goes off to play with someone else.

Take suggestions from the group. Some may not be appropriate and you should help the children to realise this. For example, 'So, Dale would be angry and want to hit the other boy. Now, the other boy is responsible for making Dale upset, but Dale would be responsible for the trouble he'd be in if he did hit him. Feeling angry doesn't have to lead to being violent.'

Cheering up
Raise your hand, palm forward, to the child on your right, who then does the same to the person on their right. This continues until the greeting has travelled round the circle.

Calming down
Ask everyone in the circle to hold hands with the person on either side of them. Choose a child to begin by gently raising and lowering the hand of the child on their left to create a wave motion. They then repeat this with the child on their left and so on until the round is completed.

Extension activities
Put the children into pairs or small groups and ask them to make a list of responses to one of the following situations:

☀ a mother tells her child to tidy their bedroom;
☀ you are walking down the corridor when someone trips over, their school bag bursts open and all their things fall out;
☀ one of your best friends is ill and away from school.

Ask for volunteers to act out some of the ways in which someone may respond in such a situation.

Explain to the children that they have been thinking about the fact that they can make choices about how they behave. Tell them that we can choose how to respond to the things that happen to us. This means that we have a responsibility to think carefully.

Ask the group to help you make a list of the things that we might need to think about when we make a choice about how we behave, such as how our choice will affect others, how it will affect ourselves, and if it will make life easier or harder for anyone. Point out that we always have a choice.

12 *We can make 'I' statements*

Key word
Responsibility: the state or position of being accountable for somebody or something

Resources
None

Meeting up
Tell the children to touch something with a part of their body, for example:

- ☀ Touch the floor with your elbow.
- ☀ Touch your teeth with your little finger.
- ☀ Touch your nose with your thumb.

Continue until everyone is attentive and ready for the next activity.

Warming up
Ask each child to complete the following sentence using the speaking object: 'I feel grown up when I . . .'.

Opening up
Recap on the work on responsibility. Introduce the idea that we need to take responsibility for the way we feel and to be able to tell others effectively. Ask your co-worker to pretend to be Ella in the following scenario:

> Stand in the middle of the circle, Ella. Now children, Ella has just won a holiday. Tell the group how you are feeling, Ella. [*Give Ella an opportunity to tell the group how she is feeling. After Ella's comments, encourage the group members to say how they are feeling.*] So, Ella is feeling very happy and excited. That's good. Well said, Ella. [*Give the members of the group a chance to respond to the happy scenario.*]

Then introduce some more difficult scenarios and ask the children to produce 'I' statements to show how they may be feeling in each case. You could try these:

- ☀ Mollie took your pencil and threw it on the floor.
- ☀ Aimee says she won't sit next to you.
- ☀ Lennox told everyone that you forgot to learn your tables.
- ☀ Marie told the teacher that you left litter on the playground.

Cheering up

Congratulate the children on their excellent work. Ask the children to suggest a positive 'We' statement to suit the occasion, such as 'We are wonderful and clever.' Follow this with a round of applause.

Calming down

Ask the children to sit on their chairs with their hands in their laps and straight backs. Ask them to close their eyes and think about their breathing. Tell them that as they breathe in, you want them to breathe in a feeling of happiness; and as they breathe out, you want them to breathe out anything that may be making them unhappy. Allow a minute or so for this. Now, ask them to imagine that they are looking through a window. They can see a picnic laid out on a lawn. They open a door and go out to enjoy the food and drink. Ask them to enjoy this picture and to open their eyes when they are ready.

Extension activities

The trouble with strong feelings is that we tend to push them on to others. Instead of making 'I' statements, we make 'You' statements, blaming other people for our problems.

Model some 'You' statements to show how aggressive and unsettling they can be. Use strong body language to intensify their impact.

☀ You are mean not to let me join in the game.
☀ You have spoiled my day by being moody.
☀ You are horrible to stop me sharing the pens.

Explain that such statements make people uneasy and cause trouble. However, if we change the words, we can explain ourselves in a way that helps us to solve a problem instead of making it worse. We do this by using an 'I' statement. By doing this, you take responsibility for the feeling and ask the other person to take responsibility for the action that caused it. This means that the previous 'You' statements might sound like this:

☀ I want you to know that I feel sad because you won't let me join in.
☀ I feel upset because you are moody and I don't understand why.
☀ I feel frustrated because I need a red pen to finish my picture.

Ask groups to make up short role plays that explore the different ways in which a situation may work out, depending on whether a 'You' or 'I' statement is used.

Social skills

13 *We understand that our actions affect other people*

Key word

Empathy: the ability to understand another person's feelings

Resources

None

Meeting up

Number the children 1 to 3 round the circle. Ask them to crouch down and balance on their hands and feet facing the centre. When you call a number, the children with that number move one of their limbs once. Call the numbers quickly. The object of the game is to cross the circle without touching anyone else, so there may need to be considerable co-operation. For example, one child may have to move backwards or sideways to allow another child to pass.

Warming up

Ask each child to complete the following sentence using the speaking object: 'I feel embarrassed when . . .'.

Opening up

Point out that we can't see thoughts and feelings because they happen inside us, but that our actions are quite different. Actions can be seen and they affect others. Talk about how you noticed that some children were helpful and moved out of the way of others in the earlier game. Explain that the game was helped by these actions. Play the game again and tell the children that you will be watching carefully for helpful behaviour.

Cheering up

If a child has done something praiseworthy during the session, commend this using verbal praise or something from your school's rewards system.

Calming down

Ask the children to sit on their chairs with their hands in their laps and straight backs. Tell them to close their eyes and to think about their breathing. Ask them to think about the following day:

> *You arrive at school and everyone smiles at you. You walk into the classroom and notice that your teacher has put your painting on the wall and it looks really good. Another teacher comes in and says she thought you behaved well in assembly. You discover you are in the team for the match on Thursday.*

Leave a short pause at the end of each sentence.

Point out that each of the people in the story used the power of action to make life feel good.

Extension activities

Ask the children to work in pairs to act out two versions of a scenario you give them or that they devise themselves, one in which someone's actions make others feel better and the other in which their actions make others feel worse.

Use mime to represent action, character or mood through gestures and movements. This helps children to learn to read body language. Background sound effects may create a heightened sense of drama.

14 *We know how to use good listening skills*

Key words
Need, help, helpful, listening, skill

Resources
None

Meeting up
Tell the children to move to various parts of the room; for example:

* ❋ Stand by the door.
* ❋ Find a chair to sit on safely.
* ❋ Stand in the centre of the circle.

Continue until everyone is attentive and ready for the next activity.

Warming up
Ask each child to complete the following sentence using the speaking object:
'My favourite sound is . . .'.

Opening up
Tell the children that you are going to look at an important way of behaving
that helps people feel cared for and happy. Ask the children to listen
carefully as you read the following rhyme:

> Robin the Bobbin,
> Just turned 10,
> Ate more food
> Than forty men.
> He ate a cow.
> He ate a calf.
> He ate an ox
> Cut in half.
>
> He ate a church
> And its steeple.
> The harvest gifts
> Brought by the people.
> A cow and a calf,
> An ox cut in half,
> A church and steeple,
> The gifts of the people.
> And yet Robin complained
> That he still wasn't full.

Ask the children what they thought of the rhyme. Explain that you could tell who was listening well without needing to ask any questions. This is because listening is something that we do with our whole body. Demonstrate this by having a conversation about your favourite foods with your co-worker. During this, your colleague needs to demonstrate a mix of good and bad listening. For bad listening, they should stare into space, yawn, interrupt and fiddle with their clothing. For good listening, they should make good eye contact, smile, nod, lean slightly forwards and make small comments as appropriate.

Ask for volunteers to talk in turn about their favourite meal. Warn them that you will use either good or bad listening skills. Ask each child if they recognised if you were listening well or not. How did they feel?

Cheering up
Name a child you think has worked well during the session. Be specific about what they did well and ask the group to wave at them cheerfully.

Calming down
Ask the children to sit on their chairs with their hands in their laps and straight backs. Ask them to close their eyes and think about their breathing. Tell them that as they breathe in, you want them to breathe in a feeling of happiness; and as they breathe out, you want them to breathe out anything that may be making them unhappy. Allow a minute or so for this. Now, ask them to imagine that they are looking through a window. They can see a mountain peak. They open a door and go out to enjoy the breathtaking views. Ask them to enjoy this picture and to open their eyes when they are ready.

Extension activities
Use a digital camera to photograph or video children during a listening activity. Ask the children to look carefully at the images and comment on what good listening skills look like.

Put the children in pairs and ask them to take turns to talk to each other about their favourite foods. As you watch them, make a note of anyone who demonstrates good listening skills. Thank the children for their good work and be specific in your praise.

15   *We know how to resist peer pressure*

Key words
Refusal skills, peer pressure

Resources
None

Meeting up
Begin this game with all the children making the same hand movement, such as small clockwise circles in front of them. Once all the children are doing this, walk round the outside of the circle and tap someone on the back. That person must count to 5 in their head and then change their hand movement. The children must be alert to spot a change. Once all the children are doing a new movement, touch another child on the back. The game continues in this way.

You might want to demonstrate some simple hand movements first to give the children some ideas.

Warming up
Ask each child to complete the following sentence using the speaking object: 'I like my friend because . . .'.

Opening up
Ask the children why it is important to stay safe. Stress that people need to stop and think before doing something that someone asks them to do. They need to think about what might happen if they do it. Sometimes they will need to say 'No', which is not always easy. Tell them that you are going to show them how to say 'No' in a calm and assertive manner. Do this by:

- ☀ standing upright;
- ☀ having your head held straight and looking forwards;
- ☀ keeping your hands relaxed and by your side;
- ☀ using a calm but firm voice.

Ask all the children to stand up and say, 'No' or 'No, thank you' firmly. Ask for confident volunteers to model this behaviour in reply to an unreasonable request, such as 'Go and tell that girl that you don't like her' or 'Let's spoil the lesson.' Explain that they may need to say 'No' in different ways and more than once. Demonstrate this with a volunteer as follows:

> 'Let's mess up the football game.'
> 'No, I don't want to get into trouble.'
> 'Oh, go on.'
> 'No, because it will make me feel bad.'
> 'We'll only do it once.'
> 'I said no.'
> 'But it will be fun.'
> 'No, I don't think it will.'

Choose relevant scenarios to practise this technique with. Explain that how we use such skills has an impact on how successful we are in lots of areas. Add that by practising such skills we'll be better able to use them in real life.

Cheering up

Perform a salaam (low bow, palm of right hand on forehead) to the child on your right, who then does the same to the person on their right. This continues until the greeting has travelled round the circle.

Calming down

Mime sunlight by slowly waving your fingers. Send this mime round the circle. Now send clouds round the circle by moving your hands, palms facing outwards, in front of your face. Finally, mime a burst of sunlight by raising your arms above your head and then folding them in front of you. Send this action round the circle.

Extension activities

Explain that it may help to name the inappropriate behaviour that they are refusing to do by saying 'No, I won't do that because it's [cheating/stealing/naughty].' Another strategy to use to avoid engaging with an inappropriate request is to change the subject.

Remind the children that they can always walk away and/or ask an adult for assistance. Role play these strategies as previously.

16   *We know how to get help when we need it*

Key word

Help: something that makes things better or makes it easier for somebody to do something

Resources

Newspaper, sticky tape, a selection of useful items such as a wooden spoon, a key, a mobile phone

Meeting up

Place an imaginary box in the centre of the circle. Ask a child to take out an imaginary object and demonstrate its use. The other children guess what it is.

When the object has been identified, everyone copies the mime and another child has a turn.

Warming up

Ask each child to complete the following sentence using the speaking object: 'I feel happiest when . . .'.

Opening up

Ask the children to choose an item and explain how it is useful. Point out that we are surrounded by things that help us get through the day. Continue the discussion by saying that we are also surrounded by people who can help us. Just as we need to learn how to use the things that help us, we also need to learn how to ask for help from people when we need it.

With your co-worker, model the most effective way of getting a teacher's attention by:

* ❋ looking at your co-worker;
* ❋ putting your hand up;
* ❋ sitting quietly;
* ❋ waiting patiently until your co-worker comes towards you;
* ❋ asking for help, remembering to say 'Please' and 'Thank you'.

Set the group the task of making a free-standing tower out of newspaper. Ask them to work as a team, helping one another and asking for help if they need it. Tell them that you will be watching for children using the skills they have learnt in this session. Afterwards, discuss how the children felt the task went. Commend any children who asked you for help and state that you were very pleased to give it.

Discuss ways in which the children might be more helpful at school and at home.

Cheering up
Teach everyone the following finger rhyme.

> A worm lives in the ground. (*wiggle fingers downwards*)
> A bird lives in a tree. (*flutter fingers upwards*)
> A fish lives in the river. (*wiggle fingers horizontally*)
> But home is the place for me! (*point to chest*)

Calming down
Remind the children of how they can calm themselves by concentrating on their breathing. Sit quietly for a few minutes practising this before softly telling them what will happen next.

Extension activities
Give members of staff who have frequent contact with the children in your group simple star charts. Ask them to reward a child with a star every time they hear them say 'Please' or 'Thank you'. Give each child a tick sheet with the names of your group on it. They can tick it every time they hear one of the others use either of these expressions. You can see how many stars each child has managed to collect by the next session. Commend them on their politeness and ask if they found life better when they used these two expressions. Get the children to say how many ticks the others achieved on the sheets they filled in.

17   *We know how to introduce ourselves*

Key words
First impression, introduce, attention, request

Resources
An empty plastic bottle, and full-body pictures of people from magazines

Meeting up
Lay the bottle down in the centre of the circle and spin it. When it stops, the child at whom the top of the bottle is pointing must talk briefly about something they really enjoy. This child then spins the bottle and the game continues.

Warming up
Ask each child to complete the following sentence using the speaking object: 'If I could go anywhere in the world, I would go to . . .'.

Opening up
Hold up one of the pictures and ask the group to comment on what they notice about the person, such as how they are dressed; whether they look friendly, boring, mean; and so on. Point out that their comments include facts (such as 'He is an old man dressed in a suit'), interpretation ('He looks tired and unhappy') and reaction ('I don't like the look of him'). Repeat with the other pictures.

Comment on how much information was collected by looking at a few pictures. Point out that each member contributed to what we call a first impression of each person. Give some examples of occasions when you formed first impressions by relating some stories of your own. These don't have to be true, but try to make them interesting. Here is an example:

> *Not long ago, I was on a train to London that was very crowded. I was sitting down, minding my own business, when this unusual character sat on the seat opposite me. He was wearing a bright red jumper and a green bobble hat and had loads and loads of luggage.*

Ask the group to contribute their own stories. Point out that these stories show that first impressions can make a big difference to how people feel about us and how they treat us.

Cheering up

Select a child who contributed well during the session. Say how pleased and happy this has made you and ask everyone to give them a round of applause. Ask the children if they noticed anyone else in the group working hard. Praise these children for their contributions.

Calming down

Mime snow by wiggling your fingers in front of you. The child on your right copies this action, and so on round the circle. When the mime reaches you, send a blizzard round the circle by rubbing your palms together. Finally, send a snow drift round by moving your feet backwards and forwards on the floor.

Extension activities

Write 'How to make a good first impression' on the flipchart. Ask the children for suggestions to write under this title. Explain that a good first impression includes how we introduce ourselves. Model how this is done, using the following:

- ❄ use a friendly facial expression;
- ❄ look directly at the other person;
- ❄ use a friendly voice as you greet them and tell them your name, 'Hello, my name is . . .'.

Put the children in pairs and ask each pair to role-play a different situation in which a good introduction would help to make a positive first impression, such as meeting a new teacher or pupil, at the dentist, playing at the park, or meeting new neighbours.

Show the children how to conclude an introduction by saying something like 'It was good to meet you. Maybe we will see each other again.'

Point out that it is a good idea to greet people whom we have known for a long time by showing our pleasure and saying 'Hello, . . .' or 'Hi, . . .'. Role-play a few scenarios to reinforce this skill.

18 *We know how to volunteer and follow instructions*

Key words
Help, helpful, volunteer

Resources
A rainstick or a recording of calm music

Meeting up
Choose a child to look at the person on their right and say 'Ha' as seriously as possible. This child then turns to the child on their right and says 'Ha Ha'. This continues round the circle, each child adding an extra 'Ha'. Anyone who laughs has to stand outside the circle and pull funny faces to try to make another child laugh. If they succeed, they swap places with that child.

Warming up
Ask each child to complete the following sentence using the speaking object: 'I like it when . . . helps me.'

Opening up
Open a discussion about how we can offer help as well as receive it. Model an effective way to volunteer by:

- ☀ making eye contact;
- ☀ using a friendly, eager voice;
- ☀ asking if you can help;
- ☀ saying 'Please';
- ☀ describing the task that you might help with;
- ☀ listening to any instructions;
- ☀ repeating them so that you are both clear about the task;
- ☀ doing what you've been asked to do straightaway;
- ☀ reporting back to the person;
- ☀ thanking them and accepting their thanks with eye contact.

Cheering up

Tell the children that you have noticed how hard some of them have been working.

Call out the names of the relevant children and talk about when you noticed them trying hard. Ask the group to give each other a cheer.

Calming down

Ask the children to sit down, close their eyes and put their hands on their knees with the palms facing upwards and their fingers lightly curled. Most children find this comfortable as it relaxes their shoulders. Use a rainstick or some gentle music to create a calm background for the children to think about what makes them special.

Extension activities

Organise some adults around the school who are willing to be helped by a group member. Agree a time for this to happen. After the activity, ask group members to describe how they got on. Make sure you feed back any positive comments you received from the adults.

Motivation

19 *We understand that we can choose to act positively when things go wrong*

Key words
Behaviour, think, choose, choice, responsibility, fable

Resources
A flipchart and a pen

Meeting up
Begin this game with all the children making the same foot movement. Once all the children are doing this, walk round the outside of the circle and tap someone on the back. That person must change their foot movement. The children must be alert to spot a change. Once all the children are doing a new movement, touch another child on the back. The game continues.

Warming up
Ask each child to complete the following sentence using the speaking object: 'When I feel sad, . . . makes me feel better.'

Opening up
Tell the group that you will be watching for how they use their listening skills while you read them the start of 'The Ant and the Pigeon'.

The Ant and the Pigeon

A thirsty ant went to the river to drink. To reach the river he had to climb down the steep river bank. Half-way down, he slipped and fell into the water. A pigeon perched in a nearby tree watched the ant fall into the water.

On the flipchart, make a list of what the pigeon might do. Explore caring and uncaring responses. Resume the story as follows:

Quickly, the pigeon dropped a leaf into the river close to the ant. The ant was able to climb onto the leaf and float safely to shore. As soon as he was on land, the ant saw a bird catcher hiding with a net in his hand. The ant realised that the pigeon was in danger.

On the flipchart, make a list of the positive and negative things the ant might do. Then continue the story as follows:

> *The ant ran up to the hunter and nipped him on the heel. The startled hunter dropped his net and the pigeon flew off. The pigeon, perched safely in another tree, called down to the ant, 'Thank you for choosing to help me.'*
>
> *'Not at all,' said the ant. 'You made a choice that helped me so I was glad to be able to help you.'*

Choose members of the group to act out the story.

Return to the lists and point out that both characters had a range of choices. Each was glad that the other thought carefully and made the right choice.

Cheering up
Touch palms with the child on your right, who then does the same with the person on their right. This continues until the greeting has travelled round the circle. End by thanking everyone for their contribution.

Calming down
Ask the children to sit on their chairs with their hands in their laps and straight backs. Ask them to close their eyes and think about their breathing. Tell them that as they breathe in, you want them to breathe in a feeling of happiness; and as they breathe out, you want them to breathe out anything that may be making them unhappy. Allow a minute or so for this. Then, ask them to imagine that they are enjoying a lovely walk on a crisp autumn day. The air is clear and the sun is shining. Ask them to enjoy this picture and to open their eyes when they are ready.

Extension activities
Make a list of situations in which things often go wrong for the children in the group. You could explore these specific problems or create similar situations for an unnamed child and ask the group to suggest helpful ways in which the person could help themselves.

If the focus is on a child in the group, they could explain their problem by saying 'I need help because . . .'. Group members can respond by saying 'Would it help if you . . .?' Give the child time to think about the suggestions, and ask them to thank everyone for their assistance. It is then possible for the group to make an action plan which the child can use in their situation.

20 *We understand how to use positive self-talk*

Key words
Think, choose, cope

Resources
Four beanbags, and two stick figures drawn on a large piece of paper – write 'I can' under one figure and 'I can't' under the other

Meeting up
Explain to the children that they are going to walk round inside the circle pretending they are on different surfaces. Start with thick mud. At intervals, call out a different surface, such as slippery ice, a trampoline, sand, hot coals, and glue.

Warming up
Ask each child to complete the following sentence using the speaking object: 'I felt proud when . . .'.

Opening up
Remind the children that they have been thinking about how they have the power to choose their actions and to calm themselves down when they need to. Ask if any of the children have used any calming techniques since the last session. Explain that they are going to look at another important skill today.

Hold up the two pictures. Point out that although the two figures look the same, they are quite different because one always thinks 'I can't' while the other always thinks 'I can.' Ask for volunteers to pretend to be the two characters. Give them a situation such as learning to juggle. Demonstrate how to do this with two beanbags. The 'I can' child then has a go at this, while the 'I can't' child sits down and doesn't bother. Ask the group who has the better chance of becoming a juggler. Write down all the skills that the 'I can' child is learning, such as throwing a beanbag, catching it, and moving the beanbag from one hand to the other. Point out that as they practise they get better. Allow the volunteers to swap roles.

Cheering up

Turn to the child on your right. Place your hands together as in prayer and bow to them. They then give the same greeting to the person on their right. This continues until the greeting has travelled round the circle.

Calming down

Ask the children to sit on their chairs with their hands in their laps and straight backs. Ask them to close their eyes and think about their breathing. Tell them that as they breathe in, you want them to breathe in a feeling of happiness; and as they breathe out, you want them to breathe out anything that may be making them unhappy. Allow a minute or so for this. Now, ask them to imagine that they are sailing on a warm sea. They can hear the sea birds overhead. Ask them to enjoy this picture and to open their eyes when they are ready.

Extension activities

Ask volunteers to share a talent they have, using the sentence 'My name is . . . and I can . . .'. Encourage them to talk about the difficulties they experienced as they learnt the skill and how they felt when they had mastered it.

Give each child a piece of paper and ask them to draw a self-portrait. They should write a list of things that they can do around their picture. Share the work with the group and celebrate the skills listed.

21 *We understand that everyone has to work towards goals*

Key words
Goal, effort

Resources
Two blindfolds, a recording of a favourite piece of music, six large pieces of paper (one with a star drawn on it), enough star badges for one for each child – these can be made from sticky paper

Meeting up
Two volunteers are blindfolded. One is the hunter and the other the quarry. The hunter needs to try to catch the quarry. The rest of the group, in a circle, guide the hunter and quarry away from the circle's edge by gently using their palms.

Warming up
Ask each child to complete the following sentence using the speaking object: 'When I'm older, I want to be . . .'.

Opening up
Play the group your chosen piece of music. Talk about who is performing it and why you like it. Ask the group to share the names of their favourite musicians and say why they like them. Ask if anyone knows what people have to do in order to become a musician. Put the pieces of paper on the floor in a line with the star at one end. Choose one child to stand at the other end of the line. Ask the children in turn to suggest what the volunteer will need to do in order to become a musician. Suggestions might include buy an instrument, take lessons, hire a manager, and sign a recording contract. The order doesn't matter at this stage. With each suggestion, the volunteer moves to the next piece of paper in the line. When they reach the star, you can play the music again and let them take a bow.

Cheering up

Congratulate the children on their interesting contributions and invite them to join you in a round of applause.

Calming down

Remind the children of how they can calm themselves down by concentrating on their breathing. Ask them to sit quietly for a few minutes practising this before quietly explaining what will happen next.

Extension activities

Give the group the opportunity to talk about some of their more immediate goals, such as to improve their handwriting, avoid fights, and learn to swim. Ask them to say 'My goal is to . . .'. The group can help each other to take steps towards that goal by offering help or advice using the following sentence stem: 'Would it help if you . . .'. Give the children a little time to think about these suggestions, and then ask them all to thank everyone else for their assistance.

Keep a note of these goals and the assistance that was offered so that you can check on progress during subsequent sessions.

22 *We understand what is helpful or unhelpful in achieving our goals*

Key words
Goal, steps
Persistence: the ability to continue steadily or obstinately despite problems, difficulties or obstacles
Quest: a search for, or a journey towards, something very important

Resources
A large piece of paper with a star drawn on it

Meeting up
Place an imaginary basket in the centre of the circle. Ask a child to take out an imaginary object from the basket and demonstrate its use. The other children guess what it is. When the object has been identified, everyone copies the mime and another child has a turn.

Warming up
Ask each child to complete the following sentence using the speaking object: 'When I was younger, I used to like . . .'.

Opening up
Introduce the idea of a quest and agree on one that interests them, such as a wizard searching for a magic potion or astronauts searching for a new planet. Choose half of the group to go on the quest. These children line up at one end of the room. Put the star at the other end. Ask the rest of the group to suggest good or bad things that might happen on the quest. For example, the astronauts might find a really fast spacecraft, only to discover that it is full of unfriendly aliens. When something helpful is suggested, the astronauts move a step towards their goal. When an obstacle is mentioned, they must take a step back. Keep going until the group reach the star. Bring the group together and talk about how achieving a goal includes facing difficulties and problems and finding ways to overcome them.

Cheering up

If any children in the group have done something worthy of praise since the last meeting, this is the time to commend their good behaviour.

Calming down

Ask the children to sit on their chairs with their hands in their laps and straight backs. Ask them to close their eyes and think about their breathing. Tell them that as they breathe in, you want them to breathe in a feeling of happiness; and as they breathe out, you want them to breathe out anything that may be making them unhappy. Allow a minute or so for this. Now, ask them to imagine that they are looking through a window. They can see a lovely park. They open a door and go out to play on the swings. Ask them to enjoy this picture. Now tell them to get themselves ready to open their eyes and to become aware of the room and today.

Extension activities

Agree on an appropriate goal for the group, such as learning their 8 times table or improving their handwriting. Ask them to think about the things that may make achieving their goal difficult. Make a wall chart to record their progress. Have a nice surprise ready for when the group reaches its goal.

23 *We know strategies to deal with frustration and disappointment*

Key words

Frustration: feeling discouraged, annoyed or weary because an aim is thwarted

Disappointment: feeling let down because something has not happened as hoped or expected

Resources

A flipchart and a pen

Meeting up

Ask the children to sit in a space on the floor. Demonstrate the following instructions:

- ☀ Alien ants – wriggle on your bottom.
- ☀ Space boots – stomp about.
- ☀ Jet pack – weave about quickly.
- ☀ Robot alert – walk like a robot.
- ☀ Anti-gravity – walk slowly as if floating.

Briskly call out instructions and ask everyone to respond as quickly as they can.

Warming up

Ask each child to complete the following sentence using the speaking object: 'I get cross when . . .'.

Opening up

Lead the group through a mime of preparing for a trip into space – putting on their spacesuit, checking the control panel, and waving goodbye. Ask volunteers to describe how they feel. Then tell them that a severe weather warning has come from Mission Control and the spaceship cannot take off today. Ask the children to mime what may follow – undressing, leaving the spaceship, and climbing into a bus, for example. Ask them to describe how they feel.

Introduce the words 'frustration' and 'disappointment' and explain that they describe the feelings just mentioned. Choose one child to pretend to be the leader of the astronauts. Tell the rest of the group that the leader needs help because they are feeling frustrated and disappointed. Tell the children that some of the work from previous sessions might be helpful. Give the group the following sentence stem and ask them to use it to help the leader: 'Would it help if . . .?' List the suggestions on the flipchart. Remind the leader to thank everyone for their helpful suggestions.

Cheering up
Comment on the good work that you saw taking place. Give the children a round of applause. Ask them to join in.

Calming down
Ask the children to sit on their chairs with their hands in their laps and straight backs. Ask them to close their eyes and think about their breathing. Tell them that as they breathe in, you want them to breathe in a feeling of happiness; and as they breathe out, you want them to breathe out anything that may be making them unhappy. Allow a minute or so for this. Then ask them to imagine that they are floating in space, taking in all its beauty. Ask them to enjoy this picture. Now tell them to get themselves ready to open their eyes and to become aware of the room and today.

Extension activities
Ask each child in turn to identify one coping strategy that they could all try when they next feel disappointed or frustrated. Write each one on a piece of card. Turn the cards over and allow one child at a time to take one. Ask them to find a partner and make up a short play to show how the strategies they have might work in practice.

24 *We know how to accept criticism*

Key words
Criticise, disapprove, dislike

Resources
Some prepared scenarios in which mild criticism is given

Meeting up
Show the children a selection of actions that correspond with visual cues. For instance:

- ☀ when you clap your hands, they stand up and wave their arms;
- ☀ when you touch your head, they hop;
- ☀ when you tap your knees, they sit down;
- ☀ when you touch your nose, they clap their hands.

Play a game using these actions.

Warming up
Ask each child to complete the following sentence using the speaking object: 'When I don't like something, I say . . .'.

Opening up
Ask the children to report back on their experience of giving and receiving praise, particularly how they felt. Explain that you are going to look at a different kind of experience, that of being criticised. Tell them about some incidents from your experience of criticism to show that it happens to everyone. Model the following appropriate behaviour for receiving criticism:

- ☀ make non-aggressive eye contact;
- ☀ stay calm;
- ☀ nod to show that you are listening;
- ☀ indicate that you have heard the person by saying 'Yes' or 'OK';
- ☀ don't argue.

Give the children opportunities to practise this behaviour in short role plays. For instance, another team member could criticise something you did. Discuss how criticism can be useful and explain that sometimes it is best to accept it, think about it and decide how to improve. However, if a person wishes to disagree with criticism, there are ways to do that which minimise problems. This can be done using the following behaviour:

- ☀ make non-aggressive eye contact;
- ☀ use a friendly, calm voice;
- ☀ tell the person that you understand how they feel;
- ☀ explain that you feel differently and give clear reasons why;
- ☀ give the other person an opportunity to reply.

Put the children in pairs or small groups and ask them to practise these behaviours using everyday school scenarios. Thank the children for their work.

Cheering up
Congratulate the children on their interesting contributions and invite them to join you in a round of applause.

Calming down
Tell the children to take a deep breath while you count to 5, then to breathe out slowly as you count down to 1. Repeat this a few times.

Extension activities
Explain that criticism can be given so that the receiver understands your disapproval but doesn't become overemotional. This can be done by using the following behaviour:

- ☀ find a place where you are unlikely to be overheard;
- ☀ make non-aggressive eye contact;
- ☀ stay calm;
- ☀ use a quiet, kind voice;
- ☀ speak in a friendly manner;
- ☀ be exact and clear about what you are criticising;
- ☀ listen to what the other person has to say;
- ☀ say something friendly so that the conversation ends in a positive way.

Give the children some scenarios. Put them in pairs or small groups and ask them to practise these behaviours using everyday school or imaginary scenarios. Thank the children for their work.

Self-esteem

25 *I know what I like about myself*

Key word
Self-esteem: positive sense of self

Resources
A beanbag, a rainstick, a recording of some calm music, a pen and some pieces of card

Meeting up
Choose a child to stand in the centre of the circle holding the beanbag. They have to make a statement such as 'My favourite food is . . .' or 'I like . . .', before naming another child and throwing the beanbag to them. They swap places and the game continues. When a child has had a turn they sit with their arms folded.

Warming up
Ask each child to complete the following sentence using the speaking object: 'My favourite drink is . . .'.

Opening up
Choose one child to sit next to you. Ask the group to make positive statements about them. Encourage them to compliment the child on their behaviour and what they do well rather than their physical appearance. Repeat each statement and rephrase it to make it even more positive, if necessary. Write the comments on a card. Continue until every child has had a turn. At the end of the session, give each child their card so that they can take it home.

Cheering up
Add your own positive comment about each child. Give your co-worker an opportunity to do likewise.

Calming down

Ask the children to sit down, close their eyes and put their hands on their knees with the palms facing upwards and their fingers lightly curled. Most children find this comfortable as it relaxes their shoulders. Use a rainstick or some gentle music to create a calm background for the children to reflect on the positive comments made about them.

Extension activities

Ask the group to make collages of things they like and their aspirations. They could cut out words or pictures from comics, magazines and newspapers that illustrate what they like or wish to become. Ask each child to hold their collage up and talk about it at the end of the activity.

26 *I know I can feel proud of myself*

Key word
Proud: the feeling of being pleased and satisfied about something that you have done or a skill that you have

Resources
None, although the children should bring in something from home that illustrates a hobby they enjoy, if possible

Meeting up
Ask each child in turn to say their name. As they do so, they must clap the rhythm of the syllables.

You could ask the rest of the group to repeat the clapping after each group member's turn.

Warming up
Ask each child to complete the following sentence using the speaking object: 'I feel happy when I hear . . .'.

Opening up
Ask each child in turn to complete the following sentence: 'My name is . . . and I . . .'.

The child then demonstrates their hobby and answers questions from the group about it.

If a child is unable to bring something from home, they can talk about something they are proud of having done at school.

Cheering up
Ask the children to stand up and chant 'We are cool.' Each time they hug themselves and pretend to shiver. They then lower their arms and repeat the sentence and action.

Calming down

Mime a breeze by tapping your fingers together. Send this mime round the circle. Now send a wind round the circle by clapping your hands together. Finally, mime the sun coming out by raising your arms above your head and then folding them in front of you. Send this action round the circle.

Extension activity

Give each child a small booklet and ask them to draw an achievement on each page. Explain that they should then write a sentence that says 'I can . . .' below each picture.

27 *We are learning to believe in ourselves*

Key word
Believe: accept as true

Resources
A rainstick or a recording of calm music

Meeting up
Explain to the children that they are going to walk round inside the circle pretending they are different animals. Ask them to start walking, then call out a kind of animal for them to mime. After a short while, call out a different kind of animal.

Warming up
Ask each child to complete the following sentence using the speaking object: 'Something that I like about myself is . . .'.

Opening up
Put the children in pairs and ask them to tell each other in turn about two small things that they have mastered recently. This could be, for instance, learning to tie their shoelaces or to spell a specific word. Bring the group together and ask each child to explain their partner's successes. Discuss the fact that very few successes happen overnight; instead they are made up of a series of steps in the right direction.

Cheering up
Commend each child for their successes. Share three cheers in a group and ask the children each to give themselves a pat on the back.

Calming down
Ask the children to sit down, close their eyes and put their hands on their knees with the palms facing upwards and their fingers lightly curled. Most children find this comfortable as it relaxes their shoulders. Use a rainstick or some gentle music to create a calm background for the children to think about their successes.

Extension activity

Give each child a large envelope and a small number of stars that are large enough for them to write their name and a sentence on. Ask each child to write their name on their envelope. Encourage them to write on one or more stars something that they have done well this week. This may be a behavioural, social or academic accomplishment. Keep the stars in the envelopes and allow the children to look at them and add to them frequently, so that even a bad week can have a brighter moment.

28 *I know I can do it*

Key words
Confidence, self-esteem

Resources
A range of classroom resources that the children use regularly

Meeting up
Choose a child to leave the room with your co-worker for a moment. Meanwhile, choose another child to be the chief. The person outside the room returns to the circle. The chief needs to devise a short series of movements, such as clapping their hands three times and stamping their feet four times. The other players must copy the chief as quickly as possible, while the person who went out tries to work out who the chief is. If the chief is found out, congratulate the child and then choose other children for the two roles. If the chief is undiscovered after a while, congratulate the children and choose two new children for the roles.

Warming up
Ask each child to complete the following sentence using the speaking object: 'My favourite activity at school is . . .'.

Opening up
Ask each member of the group to choose something that they enjoy from the selection of classroom resources. One at a time, ask them to show it to the group, explain its use and demonstrate what they do with it. Encourage group members to ask helpful questions and offer positive feedback. Praise children who show their interest in socially pro-active ways.

Cheering up
Commend each child for an aspect of their presentation. Ask the children for positive comments about the presentations of others.

Calming down

Tell everyone to hold hands and close their eyes. Name a child to swing the hand of the child on their left to and fro gently. After five swings, the child on their left then does the same to the child on their left and so on round the circle.

Extension activity

Arrange for your group to visit a class to which they present their hobbies. This will raise the children's sense of competence.

29 *We know that success comes from thinking 'I can' and not 'I can't'*

Key word
Success

Resources
A lightweight ball

Meeting up
Give the ball to a child. They say the name of another child in the circle and roll the ball to them. This continues until everyone has had a turn. The children should fold their arms once they have had their turn.

Warming up
Remind the children of the expertise they demonstrated in the previous session. Ask each child to complete the following sentence using the speaking object: 'I am good at . . .'.

Opening up
Talk about the things that members of the group are good at. Ask the children to raise their hand and state a skill they would like to master, using the following sentence stem: 'I should like to learn how to . . .'. Other group members can offer to help by saying 'Would you like me to . . .?' Ask this child if they experienced any problems when they learnt this skill and how they overcame them. Remind the group that success is likely to come from a positive attitude and perseverance.

Cheering up
Ask the children to stand up and chant 'We are special.' Each time they say 'special' they clap their hands and cheer.

Extension activities

Give the children the opportunity to be a teacher by allowing them to teach each other something. They might know some gymnastics and could lead the group in a warm-up or keep-fit session. Perhaps they could invite an adult to the group to show them their particular skill. It is good for children's self-esteem to assist an adult in this way.

30 *We know we are making progress*

Key word
Progress

Resources
Two beanbags, a rainstick or a recording of some calm music, the envelopes and stars mentioned on page 121, paper stars, pens and art materials

Meeting up
Divide the children into two teams. Mix up the players from each team in the circle. Give a beanbag to a member of each team – they should be opposite each other in the circle. On your signal, the beanbags should be passed round the circle in the same direction. However, they must only be passed to members of the relevant team. If one beanbag overtakes the other, the team with the overtaking beanbag scores a point and the game begins again. The first team to score three points wins.

Warming up
Ask each child to complete the following sentence using the speaking object: 'I felt pleased and proud when . . .'.

Opening up
Hand out the envelopes with the stars in. Ask the children to decorate the envelope. They can work individually or in pairs. Ask each child to complete another couple of stars. Ask each child to choose a star from their envelope to read to the group.

Cheering up
You and your co-worker should write a star for each child, commenting on their positive contribution to the group.

Calming down

Ask the children to sit down, close their eyes and put their hands on their knees with the palms facing upwards and their fingers lightly curled. Most children find this comfortable as it relaxes their shoulders. Use a rainstick or some gentle music to create a calm background for the children to think about what they have written on their stars.

Extension activity

Make sure the envelopes are available so that the children can look at their stars and add to them frequently. This can be a boost if they are having a bad week.

9 Two case studies incorporating circles of support

The two projects outlined in this chapter are examples of resourceful and creative small-group work currently running in schools.

Supporting children with social, emotional and behavioural needs through circles of support, by Jayne Allan, Barnados

I work as part of a team of teachers, social workers and community support workers. We work with children experiencing social, emotional or behavioural difficulties who are referred to us by headteachers. We aim to help children change their behaviour for the better. As such we work with children individually, as part of a small group and in class.

Small circles of support

On referral, an assessment of the child is carried out with the class teacher. This identifies the child's needs and targeted support is agreed. We often discover that children referred to us find it difficult to interact with their peers appropriately and struggle to co-operate with others. We find it helpful to invite such children to join a small group that includes some children with good co-operation skills, who will benefit in some way from the small-group format.

The group usually lasts for ten weeks, each session taking an hour. The rules, incentives and sanctions relate directly to the child's time within the group. The direct teaching of co-operative skills helps to clarify to the child what it means to work as part of a group. Children will strive to co-operate and display the skills being taught in a group setting. However, it may be difficult for children to transfer these skills to the classroom and playground. In such cases, I work with the class teacher, the referred child and their peers in some whole-class activities. We use Circle Time to enhance the co-operative skills of the whole class.

The outcomes of the work are positive. Referred children are often more able to work to a set of agreed rules and display co-operative skills, and can clearly and appropriately express their feelings. As a result, other children are more willing to negotiate with them and develop a positive relationship, and they benefit from the child's enhanced social skills.

A series of ten concise session plans to develop social skills

Each session begins with a focus on the agreed group rules, followed by a warm-up game. After an activity we conduct some rounds using the following sentence stems, before ending with a game:

- ☀ I was good at . . .
- ☀ I would give myself . . . out of 10 for my work today.
- ☀ Next week I will try to . . .

Session 1

This session focuses on establishing the ground rules for the group. We discuss the rules of the group and the rewards and sanctions we will use. We play a game to get to know names of group members, such as the following ball game.

> Give a ball to a child. They say the name of another child in the circle and roll the ball to them. This continues until everyone has had a turn. The children should fold their arms once they have had their turn.

Activities focus on finding out about each other. We use paired discussion followed by individuals giving feedback to the group. We also use circle games in which children swap seats based on whether they fit a category or not.

Lastly, we explore what makes a good team. We get the children to work in pairs to complete a jigsaw, praising their co-operative skills.

Session 2

After the review and warm-up game, the group is divided into small teams. Each team agrees on a group name, a group animal and a group motto. They record these in words and pictures.

Session 3

After the initial activity, team members work together to compose a simple musical accompaniment for their motto.

Session 4

The challenge in this session is for team members to work together to build a wind-powered machine using a range of construction materials. You can test the final machines outside, or inside using an electric fan.

Session 5

In this session's activity, each team has to cross an imaginary swamp. Give each team an amount of money to spend. They must bid for pieces of equipment that they would like to use to cross the swamp. These could include gym equipment such as small boxes or planks. Once they have their equipment, they must try to use it to cross the room as a team without falling into the swamp.

Session 6

We call the activity in this session the Marshmallow Olympics. Each group is given a large beanbag or floor cushion that they need to move through an obstacle course of PE equipment.

Session 7

The challenge for each team in this session is to design and make a carrier bag using a set amount of materials.

Session 8

In this session the teams are given a selection of magazines, newspapers or comics. They are then told to find specific pictures, adverts, articles or stories.

Session 9

In this session, each team, using puppets, works on a short play that explores the benefits of working together.

Session 10

In this evaluation session, the group makes a list of the activities they have done in the programme. Each child chooses five of their favourite activities. Each reviews their progress and areas for development when they return to the classroom.

A modified-curriculum group, by Helen Sonnet

This group was set up to support children who were failing in the classroom, typically children who were challenging or withdrawn. These children were able to cope in the morning in class, but it was felt that they needed small-group support in the afternoons.

The children's eligibility to attend the group and their subsequent progress was assessed using the Boxall Profile (see page 147), a diagnostic tool completed by the children's teachers which highlights the areas of concern that may cause a child's inappropriate behaviour. We also used these findings to help determine the amount of time each child spent with the group, which varied from two terms to two years.

The group offers a different timetable to up to twelve children, with the intention of giving the children a taste of success, perhaps for the first time, by raising their self-esteem, developing their learning skills and promoting good social skills. Each term has a different behavioural focus. We use motivational group incentives and individual incentives based on targets that are regularly reviewed.

An afternoon consists of the following activities displayed on a visual timetable:

- ☀ greeting;
- ☀ circle activities;
- ☀ designated activity of the day;
- ☀ free play;
- ☀ preparations for refreshments;
- ☀ drinks and biscuits;
- ☀ washing up and story time;
- ☀ clapping rhyme or song;
- ☀ ending ritual.

The greeting and circle activities are designed to promote positive group dynamics, enhance social skills and raise self-esteem.

The designated activity is a valuable opportunity to raise the children's self-esteem. Our activities include cooking, gardening, science, art, drama, team games and tactile activities. We choose activities that provide an obvious end product that will give the children a sense of achievement.

Free play enables us to observe the group's social interactions, and provides the children with an opportunity to practise the positive behaviour modelled by the adults. The adults can use this time to play with a child who is on their own.

Refreshments are prepared and tidied away by the children. Sharing in a snack and a drink is a satisfying experience for the children. This leads nicely into the final calming activities of the afternoon.

Discipline is maintained through a busy schedule and by having clear behavioural boundaries that we maintain consistently. We display the following four rules:

- ✵ We play gently.
- ✵ We talk to people politely.
- ✵ We share the toys and equipment.
- ✵ We look after the toys and equipment.

We use time out as a sanction. This is considered a fair consequence. It is immediate and they return to the group with a clean slate afterwards.

The majority of the children who have attended the group have shown improvements. In half the children, these improvements were carried over to the classroom. The greatest improvements have been with the children who were withdrawn and/or struggling academically. The former's ability to develop relationships in the group raised their confidence and helped them to participate more fully in class activities. The boost to the self-esteem of the latter resulted in improved general behaviour.

Children with emotional and behavioural problems were the most difficult to influence, but generally these children showed some improvement in their behaviour overall, particularly at lunchtimes.

The success of the group has been acknowledged by the staff in the school, and school has become a more enjoyable and rewarding experience for the children involved. For more information see **www.positiveteaching.co.uk**

10 Other projects that support children 'beyond'

There are some wonderful projects in schools that are supporting children. Some, like the Massage in Schools Programme, intervene at Wave 1. Others, like nurture groups, consist of a structured programme of small-group work at Wave 2. We also know of schools that employ trained therapists to carry out one-to-one support for children at Wave 3.

The therapeutic approaches in this chapter aim to support children in pursuing interests that can help them become more rounded personalities. Art, drama, massage, music and play are all useful therapeutic tools.

We should like to thank the practitioners who have contributed the materials in this chapter. We believe that there is no substitute for the sharing of best practice, especially when it can help us support the most challenging of children. Contact details for the organisations mentioned may be found in Chapter 13.

Massage in Schools Programme

The Massage in Schools Programme (MISP) is a whole-class intervention which we would class as a Wave-1 intervention. Using positive, beneficial and respectful touch, the programme includes the whole class in a regular, nurturing peer-massage routine that helps to enhance children's well-being.

This well-structured and simple programme for children of primary-school age was founded by Mia Elmsäter from Sweden and Sylvie Hétu from Canada in 2000. Their vision is that every child attending school should experience positive and nurturing touch every day. We believe that nurturing touch is beneficial for children on an emotional and physical level.

MISP is based on the concept of respect for self and others. It involves a daily massage routine and activities that integrate positive touch in the school curriculum. The fully clothed massage is given by a child to another child on their back, head, arms and hands. Children ask permission to do this and consider the other's feelings.

One of the programme's strengths is that it can be used in a whole-class format with the aim of promoting a whole-school approach to positive behaviour. Children recognise and are empowered by the equality and positive language promoted by the programme. MISP is a valuable way to boost self-esteem and to help to fulfil aspects of Every Child Matters.

Nurture groups

Nurture groups are an invaluable resource for children who have been unable to thrive in the mainstream classroom (see Bennathan and Boxall 2006). They provide a place for such children to grow socially and emotionally. This kind of intervention could be classed as a Wave-2 activity as it takes children out of class for small-group work.

Nurturing children within a small group, by Simon Bishop

A nurture group allows schools to provide support for children who are unable to cope in a classroom. In a nurture group there are normally no more than twelve children assisted by two adults. The days are slow moving and tightly structured, with an emphasis on routine. The room has a homely feel, with the children and adults sharing meals together.

Much of the learning that occurs in a nurture group is at the pre-school level, and is to do with looking, listening, talking, turn-taking, knowing one's self, developing an awareness of your own and others' needs, how you fit into a group, developing internalised controls, and so on. The relationships that the children have with the adults help them to change their perception of themselves. It is these positive and affirming relationships that enable a child to change how they see themselves, from being worthless to being worthwhile. As such negative thinking is addressed, the energy needed for formal learning can be developed and academic progress will begin to be made, with the child being reintegrated gradually into their class.

This is what a typical day in our nurture group looks like:

09.00 – 09.40	Registration, sharing, circle activities, singing, preparing breakfast
09.40 – 10.45	Breakfast, assembly, playtime
10.45 – 11.05	Literacy
11.05 – 11.20	Free-choice activities
11.20 – 11.40	Maths
11.40 – 12.00	Free-choice activities
12.00 – 12.15	Circle Time
12.15 – 1.15	Lunch
1.15 – 1.30	Reading
1.30 – 2.30	Monday: games outside; Tuesday: art; Wednesday: visit/trip; Thursday: cooking; Friday: in class
2.30 – 2.45	Music / Circle Time / story
2.45	Return to class

Working with therapists

Some schools bring in trained practitioners and therapists to carry out specialist intervention work. The first section below focuses on the programme called 'A Quiet Place', in which psychotherapy is one of the key elements of a broader intervention. The work in the second section was carried out on a one-to-one basis by a psychotherapist.

A Quiet Place, by Penelope Moon

A Quiet Place is a rigorously monitored and evaluated programme designed to help children to change their behaviour. The programme consists of three key parts:

- ✳ An emotional-intelligence curriculum, delivered by a trained facilitator.
- ✳ Bodywork – using touch to support and nurture change, delivered by a qualified therapist.
- ✳ Management of feelings – understanding of the physiology of emotion through a biofeedback programme called HeartMath, which is also a stand-alone module, delivered by a trained person in the school.

Children can be referred to us by teachers or by parents or carers and, in some cases, the children refer themselves. We liaise with parents or carers, the teacher and the child to identify a desired outcome based on the child's emotional well-being. In addition to providing individual case support, the whole school benefits from a programme of small-group relaxation, the use of stories and Breathing Space training – a form of Circle Time. We also use peer massage, peer mentoring and reflective parenting programmes that develop once the individual programme has had time to bed down.

A Quiet Place is an inclusive and holistic approach with traditional and complementary techniques that support all involved in a partnership for change.

Psychotherapy in schools, by Shannon Woolf

The use of metaphor is an invaluable tool for therapeutic intervention with children as it enables them to communicate naturally and instinctively, providing insights into their internal world and thought processes. My work is to interpret these subtle clues, inviting connections with the inner self of the child. Art, storytelling and imagery are particularly helpful with children as they engage readily with such media.

I have used clay in this way before when working with an 11-year-old girl who had been referred for her anti-social behaviour. She appeared to have a blasé attitude towards most things. Knowing that clay stimulates the tactile and kinaesthetic senses, I felt it appropriate to introduce it during one of our sessions. I felt this might enable her to express herself more freely. After handling the clay, she informed me that she wanted to make a turtle, which I encouraged her to do.

On reflection, I realised that she was probably showing herself via the turtle as having a hard outer shell to shield her from the world, while inwardly displaying a more vulnerable and sensitive side of her personality, which she occasionally allowed others to see. This insight and concept of self helped in later sessions.

Creative visualisations

One powerful technique that can be used sensitively by anyone working with children is creative visualisation. This technique can be used with the whole class at Wave 1, with small groups at Wave 2 or individually as part of a Wave-3 therapeutic intervention programme. An explanation of how this powerful technique can be used to best effect follows.

Visualisation in children's lives, by Maggie Dent

Although mental rehearsal has been around for a long time, it is not something that has been taught to children. I believe this is because it is difficult to analyse and so has been seen as dubious. Thankfully, recent research into the brain's functioning has supported the power of visualisation. Read through and then try the following exercise.

> **Stand with your feet comfortably apart. Raise your left arm in front of you. Then turn slowly to the left, keeping your feet still and following your arm as far as is comfortable. Look along your arm at what your fingers are pointing at. This is point 1. Then, without moving your arm, continue moving your head until you are looking at a point approximately 60 cm beyond it. This is point 2.**
>
> **Return to the starting position and close your eyes. Now, imagine repeating the exercise. Imagine lifting your left arm, turning slowly and, when you get to point 1, imagine effortlessly passing that point and lining your arm up at point 2. Imagine that it is easy and that you are lined up to a place much further than you were on your first attempt. Imagine returning to the start position. Now open your eyes and repeat the actual exercise. Where does your arm point to now? Most people's will be lined up to point 2.**

This is an attempt to show that we can change our performance when we change our inner perception. If we can see it with the mind then the chances that the body will follow are much better. Our brain cannot distinguish between real and vividly imagined images. They both seem real and so the body will think they are real. That is why a healthy imagination from early childhood is important. Can you see the implications for children who are underachieving or lacking in social skills?

I have seen hundreds of children and teenagers over the last ten years who have the worst possible vision of themselves. Often an inner voice criticised or reinforced negative messages they heard when younger. They used positive visualisations to quieten their conscious and subconscious minds so that they could hear some positive messages about themselves (see Dent 2003).

The increasing rates of sleep deprivation, hyperactivity and anxiety disorders in our children are a deep concern for anyone who works with them. Creative visualisation can assist these children to overcome some of these symptoms. The reassurance that comes from using creative visualisation goes deep within the psyche as it is being heard without being filtered by the ego. Now, more than ever, our children need to be reminded that they have great potential, no matter what they have done so far.

Managing stress, uncertainty and fear are key areas in building resilience. Without healthy coping strategies many young people resort to difficult behaviour, withdraw or drown in their own emotion. Teaching children the positive power of healthy imaginings will give them a tool to help them become the best that they can be.

11 Looking after yourself and your colleagues

Research has shown that children are affected by their teachers' levels of self-esteem, and that teachers with low self-esteem are more likely than others to have children in their class with low self-esteem. Common sense suggests a problem of co-dependence. The kindest thing that you can do for a child is to look after yourself. Failure to do that is the main obstacle to your being the person you need to be in the classroom.

Many of us think that we do not have time to care for ourselves or that we should be giving more time to our partner, our family or our friends, and we put ourselves at the bottom of the list. The ones hurt most by this in your professional life are the children you work with, as you tend to over-react to anything difficult that they do. This is a good indication that you have lost your perspective.

The checklist on page 142 will help you identify if you are not looking after yourself properly. If a lot of your answers are 'Could do better', that suggests you need to assess your practice and that the school may need to review some of its systems.

Creating a work–life balance

Your levels of energy, stress, self-esteem and self-confidence are inextricably linked with your ability to enjoy life and to be positive, creative and efficient. When there is too much work piled upon us and we feel exceptionally stressed, our energy may decrease until we are affected both emotionally and physically. If this occurs for a prolonged period of time, we suffer.

Work–life balance is an area that is increasingly receiving attention, and although it is beyond the scope of this book we do urge you to consider this as an important part of any strategies that you think about implementing.

Whole-staff strategies

We have often been in staffrooms where everyone is too busy to know how everyone else is getting along. At worst, staffrooms can be fairly hostile environments. There is a checklist on page 143 to help you assess mutual esteem in your staffroom.

Consider your responses to the questions and decide if it is time for some reflection upon the working atmosphere within the school. In-service training days provide opportunities to work together and discuss what everyone's needs are. However, they need careful and sensitive facilitation. The checklist on page 144 will give you some ideas to make sure the school creates a caring environment for the staff.

The use of individual supervision

'Supervision' is the term for a formal support process that practitioners working with clients in social services, the health service and children's services often receive as part of their work. It mostly takes the form of a confidential dialogue about the practitioner's work with a supervisor. It is a dynamic relationship that helps the practitioner to take time to reflect, become aware of their own personal development and share any concerns or issues that might otherwise remain unvoiced. Supervision is a powerful tool in the social services and in mental-health-related fields. In education it has been neglected, along with the mental health of the adult practitioners.

We wonder how is it that teachers, who are often dealing with damaged individuals, are never given time on a weekly basis with a peer mentor, counsellor or line manager to focus on the issues that are getting in the way of their being the best they can be.

For a team to be safe enough to work with unhappy children in a way that is supportive and open, we strongly recommend that they should be practising Circle of Support as a group. In the 1930s circle meetings began to be introduced in industry to help individuals raise issues within a team environment. Unfortunately, the meetings frequently became no more than moaning sessions and had very little influence on policies or strategies. The initiative amounted to no more than cosmetic listening. If listening is to be a dynamic force, key people must be selected to take ideas from the group to the policy-making stakeholders. Your staff Circle Time needs to be an effective listening system and a forum for change for all staff in the school.

Coming full circle

The Quality Circle Time model has a strong emphasis on the emotional health and well-being of the adults in a school community. We believe that it is important that staff members create a group care plan through a staff social committee. If this is not possible, staff should be supported as they each develop a personal care plan. If you get too tired, you can become insensitive. However, if you boost your energy, you are more likely to be able to keep a sense of perspective. The most important person you need to be kind to is yourself.

Key points

★ Research shows that children are affected by their teachers' levels of self-esteem. Children with teachers who have low self-esteem are more likely to have low self-esteem themselves.

★ It will benefit you and the children you teach if you look after yourself as best you can, reducing your stress levels to help you deal with the challenges that you face every day in school.

★ We recommend that all staff teams working with children 'beyond' should meet regularly for Circle Time.

★ Energy levels and self-esteem have a direct impact on creativity and ability to enjoy life. We recommend that all teaching staff regularly reflect on their work–life balance to see if there are any improvements that can be made.

★ Many practitioners who care for people with mental and emotional health difficulties receive supervision. This is not common among teachers, who often play a key role in the lives of children with severe emotional problems.

★ One way of taking care of the children in your class and of yourself is to have your Wave-1 systems in place and working. When these systems are running smoothly, valuable classroom time and energy will be gained.

Looking after yourself

	Yes	Could do better	Action plan
Do you make sure you have the essentials for life every day – nourishing food, enough sleep, plenty of water to drink, fresh air and exercise?			
Have you learnt how to calm yourself down when you need to – breathing deeply, thinking calm thoughts?			
As time management is important, do you spend time planning how to organise your day – both in work and outside it?			
Are you clear about your rights and responsibilities within your job?			
Are you aware that there are people to talk to if you come across particular difficulties in your work?			
Are you assertive enough to say 'No' when you need to?			
Have you learnt that handling criticism is part of your job, and that the fact that you can never please all the people all of the time does not make you a poor practitioner?			
Do you have a clear understanding of your personal and professional priorities?			
Are you are working towards a more fulfilling existence?			
Have you thought about ways to make your professional and private life better, and have you implemented a few changes?			
Do you allow yourself some leisure time in which you do what you enjoy and what nourishes you?			

Assessing the mutual esteem and behaviour of staff

	Yes	Could do better	Action plan
Do the staff go to the staffroom because it has a pleasant atmosphere and it is easy to relax there?			
Are staff supportive of each other and thoughtful about each other's work needs?			
Do the staff have opportunities to put forward their views on school issues?			
Are put downs that are used as a means of criticism dealt with effectively?			
Is the staffroom relatively free of sarcasm, cynicism and negativity?			
Do the staff have time to reflect upon their successes, either informally or in staff meetings?			
Do the staff arrange social occasions in which they relax and enjoy each other's company?			
Do the staff feel able to consult each other about their problems?			
Are senior members of staff approachable and helpful?			
Do the staff complain a lot about their workload and responsibilities?			

Is your school offering its staff a caring environment?

	Yes	Could do better	Action plan
Are there timetabled staff Circle Time meetings at which staff can ask for support with troubled children?			
Is there a notice board in the staffroom for positive comments and feedback?			
Is the staffroom an attractive place to unwind?			
Do the staff remember to celebrate successes, birthdays, end of term, and so on?			
Is there a notice board where inspirational comments and quotes can be displayed?			
Are there termly staff meetings to devise ways to keep morale high?			
Do staff get together to discuss work–life balance and agree on measures to make their lives easier?			
Are staff facilities made as aesthetically pleasing as possible?			

12 Assessing, evaluating and monitoring progress

The measurement of value and change

Change can be really difficult to measure – especially changes in attitude, behaviour, emotional literacy and resilience. Often teachers will be able to identify pupils who will be helped by a Circle of Support by using knowledge, experience and intuition, and will then design sessions to maximise the benefit that the children will receive from attending. However, in some situations you may want to evaluate what you are doing for your own benefit or someone else's.

It is worth thinking through the following purposes of assessment:

- ☀ Formative assessment – sharing simple 'I can' statements with the children, and allowing them to assess themselves against these in order to celebrate successes and identify the next target.
- ☀ Summative assessment – reporting on absolute achievements and scores for evaluative or accountability purposes. For this type of assessment, a standardised, reliable measuring tool is required.

Your school SENCo may use a system of assessment that would suit your purposes. It may be possible to link your learning outcomes and success criteria with the PSHE and Citizenship curriculum, or with other social, emotional and behavioural curricula that your school or education authority uses.

There are other evaluation systems and questionnaires that you might use. Some of the following suggestions may fit your circumstances.

The Mosley Behaviour Questionnaire for Pupils, Teachers and Parents/Carers

This comprises separate sets of questions for pupils, staff and parents or carers. The questions are devised so that cross-comparisons can be made between the answers. You could discuss the questions with children during Circle Time. For younger children or those with reading difficulties, it is best to discuss the questions and to work through them individually. A modified version of the questionnaire is to be found at the end of this chapter (page 151).

The questionnaires are not validated. However, the answers given can be useful for seeing whether those completing them have a sense of where they are in terms of behaviour. If the child's responses match up to the teacher's in some areas, it will be clear that the former has a good sense of their issues. You can then discuss with the child the changes that they might make that will help them.

If there is a mismatch between the adult's responses and the child's, the first thing the child is likely to need is opportunities to increase their self-knowledge and self-perception. If you think that the mismatch is due to a personality clash between the child and their teacher, see if another adult could complete the teacher's questionnaire to see if this changes things.

Each questionnaire is divided into the following three sets of questions.

Set A – behaviour characterised by a lack of self-control

If between five and ten answers in this area are 'often' or 'always', this is a signal that the child needs help with moving towards an inner locus of control. They need to have more conscious control over their own behaviour. Learning about cause and effect, consequences and empathy will all help the child to move forward.

Set B – withdrawn behaviour

If between five and ten answers in this area are 'often' or 'always', the suggestion is that the child is unhappy and withdrawn. They may have given up trying to get their needs met. The approach that will help these children will be one that focuses on nurture, trust, positive self-image and self-esteem. Speaking and listening will be an important part of the work as they need to know that their voice can be heard and can have an impact. Children with withdrawn behaviour can benefit from playing games in which they are part of a team, and from teaching other children.

They may suffer from learned helplessness and need help to get back on their own feet. Children in this category may be at risk of self-harm or have moved towards elective mutism. If they are very withdrawn, one hour a week in a Circle of Support will not be enough. Ideally, they will receive help from a nurture group or one-to-one psychotherapy.

Set C – hostile behaviour and the deliberate choosing of poor behaviour

If between five and ten answers in this area are 'often' or 'always', the suggestion is that the child will need to make changes to help their self-esteem and self-view. They may need anger management and behavioural support. If they are addicted to failure, they will need help in finding meaningful achievement within their activities.

In all three sections self-esteem is the lowest common denominator, in that it underpins work in all the areas of need for these children. With the first set of questions, the child is not aware of their behaviour and is operating from an outer locus of control. In the second set, the child has gone within themselves and is behaving in a withdrawn way. In the third set, the child is operating from an inner locus of control in that they are responding negatively to a situation to get their needs met.

The Boxall Profile

The highly praised Boxall Profile was developed by Marjorie Boxall and her colleagues, and is aimed at primary-age children. It is the chief assessment tool of nurture groups and it has been widely used and validated. It is specifically designed to assess pupils with emotional and behavioural difficulties so that teachers can plan focused intervention. It is very easily usable and it provides a framework for the structured observation of children in the classroom (Bennathan and Boxall 2006).

Goodman's Strengths and Difficulties Questionnaire (SDQ)

For evaluative purposes, this is a widely used and validated brief behavioural screening questionnaire designed by Robert Goodman. The questionnaire will help to identify the most needy children objectively, and is suitable for pre- and post-assessment. It consists of twenty-five psychological attributes, some positive and some negative. The different areas covered by the questions are: emotional symptoms, conduct problems, hyperactivity and inattention, peer relationship problems and pro-social behaviour. The scores for each area are added together to generate a total difficulties score. One of the great advantages of this assessment is that there are different versions to cover different age groups, and specific versions for researchers, clinicians and educationalists. The website for this assessment is **www.sdqinfo.com** (Goodman 1999).

The Harter Self-perception Profile for Children

The Self-perception Profile for Children has been used as a measuring tool by many researchers. It consists of a series of statements that children agree or disagree with. It was designed for use in mainstream education and has been well validated as a measure of self-perception and self-esteem. The questionnaire taps into children's judgements of their own characteristics to provide a score for their 'global self-worth' – a term used by Harter that could be described as self-esteem (Harter 1985).

Pupil View Questionnaire

The most sturdy measurement tools are often developed within research centres, such as the Centre for Learning and Teaching, University of Newcastle. One questionnaire has been used across a group of schools in the Campaign for Learning's Learning To Learn project. This long-term project is looking at aspects of how pupils can be enabled to learn effectively so that each has the best chance to achieve their full potential. The action research project can be found, at the time of writing, on the Campaign for Learning's website: **www.campaign-for-learning.org.uk**

Draw and Write

Draw and Write or Drawing and Dialogue is a technique for accessing a child's self-perception ideas. The child is asked to draw in response to a request such as 'Draw yourself being happy.' They are asked to write some words related to the drawing, or to talk about it. The drawing is not analysed, but it is used as a focus for thoughts on the subject that are then written down or spoken. Noreen Wetton has worked with children using this technique, and gained information that was used to help design health-education programmes for primary schools. This technique is extremely useful for revealing children's unique perceptions of the situations in which they find themselves, although it is most effective when experienced practitioners use it. This is due to the importance of asking the more pertinent questions (Williams and Wetton 2000).

NfER Nelson Emotional Literacy – Assessment and Intervention

The NfER Nelson Emotional Literacy Assessment can be used with primary and secondary pupils. It has been standardised. It helps to identify a pupil's emotional-literacy status, covering such areas as emotional resilience, self-awareness, motivation and handling emotions and relationships.

One benefit of using this assessment tool is that it also provides age-appropriate follow-up intervention activities. It allows for reassessment, so practitioners can monitor progress. This resource is only available to schools or registered test users. Visit **www.nfer-nelson.co.uk** for more information.

Affirmative statements

Instead of completing a questionnaire, children can be asked to agree or disagree with sets of positive statements, such as 'I feel good when I have finished my work.' There are ready-made sets of such statements in the SEAL documentation that would work well. We have included some sets of affirmative statements on pages 154–156. These statements have been based on the five strands of the SEAL materials – self-awareness, managing feelings, motivation, empathy, and social skills – with the addition of a section on resilience, an area we feel is important for children 'beyond'.

The statements on pages 154–156 have not been validated. However, they provide a useful means by which children can judge how they are getting on and what they may want to work on next. They are not intended as a means to identify children who need additional support, or to evaluate any support a child may already be receiving.

If you need a validated tool you should refer to one of the other assessment tools mentioned previously.

Key points

★ Change in children's attitude, behaviour, emotional development and self-esteem may be hard to measure.

★ Practitioners may wish to assess their practice and to measure change to help support their work, to assist with applications for funding, or to show other staff the progress their project is making.

★ There are a number of research tools and methods available. You should first find out if your school uses a specific method already.

★ There are many assessment tools, some of which we mention.

The Mosley Behaviour Questionnaire for pupils

		(Nearly) Never	Rarely	Sometimes	Often	(Nearly) Always	
Name:							
Date:							
1.	Do you go into class late and play around outside the classroom?						A
2.	Do you call out in lessons?						
3.	Do you forget the things you need to bring to school?						
4.	Do you find it hard to concentrate if the teacher asks you to do something?						
5.	Do you get fidgety when you are trying to do something?						
6.	If a teacher asks you about the work you are doing, do you find you have forgotten what it was about?						
7.	Do you find it hard to do your work and make decisions on your own?						
8.	Do you feel clumsy and bump into things and drop things a lot?						
9.	Do you bother other children in your class when you should be working?						
10.	Do you get out of your seat during lessons when you're not supposed to?						
1.	Do you sit on your own unless the teacher asks you to sit next to someone?						B
2.	Do you avoid putting your hand up in class?						
3.	Do you worry if a teacher asks you a question?						
4.	Do you feel unhappy in school?						
5.	Do you worry about what other children think of you?						
6.	Do you find it hard to feel confident?						
7.	Do you feel you are on your own at school?						
8.	Are you in the wrong place in school sometimes – in the playground when you should have come in, or in the corridor when you should be in class?						
9.	Do you try not to look at people when you talk to them?						
10.	Do you feel embarrassed if someone says some good things about you?						
1.	If another child does well, do you say something unkind to them?						C
2.	If the teacher asks you a question, do you try not to answer?						
3.	If a teacher tells you off, do you answer back?						
4.	When you are given instructions for how to do something, do you ignore them and do what you want to do?						
5.	Do you ever jog people's elbow or chair deliberately?						
6.	Do you get angry and hit out at the teacher or children?						
7.	Do you take other people's things and hide them or spoil them?						
8.	Do you try to disrupt other children in lessons?						
9.	Do you screw up your work or scribble on it if your teacher says it is good?						
10.	When you are asked to sit down, do you get up and walk around?						

The Mosley Behaviour Questionnaire for teachers

		(Nearly) Never	Rarely	Sometimes	Often	(Nearly) Always
Name of pupil: **Name of teacher:** Date:						
A Behaviour characterised by lack of self-control, self-management or self-care	1. Arrives late in class and messes around outside the classroom before coming in.					
	2. Calls out loudly and repeatedly during lessons.					
	3. Forgets things needed for lessons.					
	4. Finds it hard to concentrate when given instructions.					
	5. Starts to fidget after a short while when given a task.					
	6. If asked about the work they are doing, they cannot respond accurately.					
	7. Finds it hard to work independently and to make decisions.					
	8. Physically clumsy, bumps into things, drops things.					
	9. Disturbs other children who are working.					
	10. Is often out of their seat during a lesson.					
B Withdrawn behaviour	1. Sits alone or has to be put beside a partner.					
	2. Does not volunteer information, put up hand or ask for clarification.					
	3. If directly questioned, looks embarrassed, and may blush or fidget.					
	4. Looks unhappy.					
	5. Is often the focus of other people's derisory or uncomplimentary comments.					
	6. Body posture is stooped or awkward.					
	7. Seems isolated in the playground and around the school.					
	8. Is often in the wrong place or somewhere at the wrong time.					
	9. Eyes are downcast and they are unable to sustain eye contact with others.					
	10. Finds it difficult to accept praise or rewards.					
C Hostile behaviour	1. They say something unkind to a child who has been praised.					
	2. If asked a question, they try not to answer it.					
	3. If told off, they answer back.					
	4. When given instructions, they ignore them and do what they want.					
	5. They jog other children's elbow or chair on purpose.					
	6. They may get angry and lash out at adults or other children.					
	7. They take other people's belongings and hide or spoil them.					
	8. They try to disrupt other children in lessons.					
	9. They screw up or deface their own work if it is praised.					
	10. When asked to sit down, they get up and walk around.					

The Mosley Behaviour Questionnaire for parents/carers

		(Nearly) Never	Rarely	Sometimes	Often	(Nearly) Always	
Name of child: Name of parent/carer: Date:							
1.	Usually late.						A. Behaviour characterised by lack of self-control, self-management or self-care
2.	Shouts out when you want quiet.						
3.	Forgetful.						
4.	Finds it hard to concentrate when you are giving instructions.						
5.	Finds it hard to settle down to do something and gets very fidgety.						
6.	When in the middle of doing something, forgets what it is about.						
7.	Does not like to do things alone or to make decisions.						
8.	Physically clumsy, bumps into things.						
9.	Tries to distract other people from what they are doing.						
10.	Is often not doing what they should be doing.						
1.	Often likes to be alone and do things alone.						B. Withdrawn behaviour
2.	Reluctant to talk much about what happens at school.						
3.	Does not like answering your questions – blushes or gets embarrassed.						
4.	Looks unhappy.						
5.	May be the victim of other children's unkind comments.						
6.	Often stooped or awkward when moving.						
7.	Prefers to play alone, even when other children are around.						
8.	Is often in the wrong place, or somewhere at the wrong time.						
9.	When talking to you, looks away, finds it hard to look you in the eye for long.						
10.	Finds it hard to take being praised or given rewards.						
1.	Finds it hard to deal with other children being praised.						C. Hostile behaviour
2.	If you ask them a question, they try not to answer.						
3.	If you tell them off, they often answer you back.						
4.	When given instructions, they ignore them and do what they want.						
5.	They jog other children's elbow or chair on purpose.						
6.	They may get angry and lash out at other people.						
7.	They take other people's things and spoil or hide them.						
8.	They try to disrupt other children.						
9.	They don't like things they do well to be praised.						
10.	When asked to calm down or sit down, they will get up and walk around.						

Permission to Photocopy

Affirmative statements

Put a tick under the number that reflects how much you agree with each statement;
1 means strongly agree and 4 means strongly disagree.

Being aware of me (self-awareness)	1	2	3	4
I am happy being me.				
People are usually fair to me.				
I break the rules sometimes.				
I behave well.				
I know that what I do affects other people.				
My friends are good to me.				
I feel I belong in school.				
Things usually turn out well for me in the end.				
I look after other people and they look after me.				
I usually know why I get upset and why I am sometimes happy.				

My feelings	1	2	3	4
I know what it is like to feel happy.				
I know what it is like to feel sad.				
I know what it is like to feel angry.				
I know how I am feeling now.				
I can cope when things go wrong.				
When I am angry I do not break things or shout or hit out.				
I can explain to other people how I am feeling.				
I know what to do to make me feel better if I get upset.				
I know how to cheer myself up if I am sad.				
I can calm myself down when I want to.				

My motivation	1	2	3	4
I look forward to coming to school.				
I have some favourite things I like doing at school.				
I feel proud of my work.				
I feel good when I play games and do sports.				
Playing with my friends makes me feel good.				
I like to do as well as I can.				
How well I do matters to me.				
I like to make things.				
I get excited when we are going out somewhere.				
Doing my best is important to me.				

How caring I am (showing empathy)	1	2	3	4
I try to cheer people up when they are upset.				
I am a caring person.				
I can easily understand how other people are feeling.				
When people feel happy, that makes me happy too.				
How other people are feeling matters to me.				
I am happy that we are all different.				
I know that some people need special help when they are not feeling OK.				
When I am upset I usually tell someone.				
I like it when we all look out for each other in school.				
Everyone should try to look after others.				

How I get on with other people (social skills)	1	2	3	4
People think I am friendly.				
I prefer to play or sit with others.				
I like talking to other people.				
I do not hit out when I am upset.				
I know how to explain things to people.				
I like working in a group and doing activities with the whole class.				
I know how to be polite.				
I try to listen to other people.				
I do not worry about whether people like me.				
Some of my friends know me very well.				

Coping with things (resilience)	1	2	3	4
I can cope with nearly everything.				
Things do not upset me a lot.				
When I am upset I soon feel better.				
I do not often worry about things.				
I get over things quickly.				
If things are stressful, I can manage.				
I am a calm person.				
If someone upsets me, I can forgive them.				
I can talk to someone about things if I am upset.				
My life is upsetting sometimes, but mostly it is great.				

13 Resources

Select bibliography

Bandura, A. (1977) *Social Learning Theory*. Upper Saddle River NJ: Prentice Hall

Bennathan, M. and M. Boxall (2006) *The Boxall Profile: Handbook for Teachers* (No.7). Network Group: London

Birkett, V. (2005) *How to Manage and Teach Children with Challenging Behaviour*. Cambridge: LDA

Cooper, P., C.J. Smith and G. Upton (1994) *Emotional and Behavioural Difficulties: Theory into Practice*. London: Routledge

Dent, M. (2003) *Saving our Children from our Chaotic World: Teaching Children the Magic of Silence and Stillness*. Australia: Pennington Publications

DfES (2003a) *Every Child Matters: the Green Paper*. Nottingham: DfES Publications

DfES (2003b) *Excellence and Enjoyment: A Strategy for Primary Schools*. Nottingham: DfES Publications

Erricker, C., J. Erricker, D. Sullivan, C. Ota and M. Fletcher (1997) *The Education of the Whole Child*. London: Cassell

Gardner, H. (1983) *Frames of Mind: The Theory of Multiple Intelligences*. Basic Books: New York

Glasser, W. (1965) *Reality Therapy: A New Approach to Psychiatry*. New York: HarperCollins

Glasser, W. (1975) *Schools without Failure*. New York: HarperCollins

Glasser, W. (1998) *The Quality School*. New York: HarperCollins

Goleman, D. (1996) *Emotional Intelligence: Why it Can Matter more than IQ*. London: Bloomsbury

Goodman, R. (1999) 'The extended version of the Strengths and Difficulties Questionnaire as a guide to child psychiatric caseness and consequent burden.' *Journal of Child Psychology and Psychiatry*, 40, 5

Harter, S. (1985) *Manual for the Self-perception Profile for Children*. Denver: University of Denver

Hawkins, P. and R. Shohet (2000) *Supervision in the Helping Professions*. Buckingham: Open University Press

Maslow, A.H. (1954) *Motivation and Personality*. New York: Harper and Row

Mead, G.H. (1934) *Mind, Self and Society*. Chicago: University of Chicago Press

Meichenbaum, D. (1977) *Cognitive-behavior Modification: An Integrative Approach*. New York: Kluwer Academic/Plenum Publishers

Mosley, J. (1988) 'Some implications arising from a small-scale study of a circle-based programme initiated for the tutorial period.' *Pastoral Care*, June 1988

Mosley, J. (1991) 'An evaluative account of the working of a dramatherapy peer support group within a comprehensive school.' *Support for Learning*, 6, 4

Mosley, J. (2006) *Step-by-Step Guide to Circle Time*. Trowbridge: Positive Press

Mosley, J. and M. Tew (1999) *Quality Circle Time in the Secondary School: A Handbook of Good Practice*. London: David Fulton

Newton, C. and D. Wilson (1999) *Circle of Friends*. Dunstable: Folens

Rogers, C. (1961) *On Becoming a Person: A Therapist's View of Psychotherapy.* Boston: Houghton Mifflin

Rogers, C. (1970) *Carl Rogers on Encounter Groups.* New York: Harper and Row

Taylor, G. (1996) 'Creating a circle of friends: a case study' in H. Cowie and S. Sharp (eds.) *Peer Counselling in School.* London: David Fulton

Taylor, G. (1997) 'Community building in schools: developing a circle of friends.' *Educational and Child Psychology*, 14

Williams, D.T. and N. Wetton (2000) *Health for Life: Ages 4–7.* Cheltenham: Nelson Thornes

Useful organisations

All Round Success
(Registered Charity no. 1064740)
28A Gloucester Road, Trowbridge,
Wiltshire, BA14 0AA
01225 767157

Anti-bullying Network
Moray House School of Education,
University of Edinburgh, Holyrood Road,
Edinburgh, EH8 8AQ
0131 651 6103; www.antibullying.net

Antidote
3rd Floor, Cityside House, 40 Adler Street,
Aldgate, London, E1 1EE
020 7247 3355; www.antidote.org.uk

Campaign for Learning
19 Buckingham Street, London, WC2N 6EF
020 7930 1111;
www.campaign-for-learning.org.uk

Caspari Foundation
Caspari House, 1 Noel Road, The Angel,
Islington, London, N1 8HQ
020 7704 1977; www.caspari.org.uk

Centre for Child Mental Health
2–18 Britannia Row, London, N1 8PA
020 7354 2913;
www.childmentalhealthcentre.org

Centre for Learning and Teaching
University of Newcastle, NE1 7RU
0191 222 5594; www.ncl.ac.uk

Esteem Plus
PO Box 389, Nedlands, 6009, Western Australia
+61 08 9822 1505; www.maggiedent.com

Institute for Arts in Therapy and Education
2–18 Britannia Row, London, N1 8PA
020 7704 2534; www.artspsychotherapy.org

Jenny Mosley Consultancies
28A Gloucester Road, Trowbridge,
Wiltshire, BA14 0AA
01225 767157; www.circle-time.co.uk

Massage in Schools Association
Acorn House, 74–94 Cherry Orchard Road,
Croydon, CR9 6DA
020 8681 8339;
www.massageinschoolsassociation.org.uk

NASEN and the British Journal of Special Education
Nasen House, 4–5 Amber Business Village,
Amber Close, Amington, Tamworth,
Staffordshire, B77 4RP
01827 311500; www.nasen.org.uk

The Nurture Group Network
004 Spitfire Studios, 63–71 Collier Street,
London, N1 9BE
020 7833 9603; www.nurturegroups.org

Positive Press Ltd
28A Gloucester Road, Trowbridge,
Wiltshire, BA14 0AA
01225 767157; www.circle-time.co.uk

Positive Teaching
11 Delmore Road, Frome, Somerset, BA11 4EG
01373 465708; www.positiveteaching.co.uk

A Quiet Place Ltd
26 Hope Street, Liverpool, L1 9BX
0151 708 6910; www.aquietplace.co.uk

Social Emotional and Behavioural Difficulties Association
Church House, 1 St Andrew's View, Penrith,
Cumbria, CA11 7YF
01768 210510; www.sebda.org

YoungMinds
48–50 St John Street, London, EC1M 4DG
020 7336 8445; www.youngminds.org.uk

Training available from Jenny Mosley Consultancies

Jenny Mosley's whole-school Quality Circle Time model is now well established and welcomed by thousands of schools throughout the UK. In recent years it has been adopted in many countries. The ease with which the model has been transferred to different cultures is an indication of the universal psychology underpinning the method.

The following courses are available from our team of highly qualified and experienced consultants:

- ❋ Create happier lunchtimes and playtimes – a whole-school approach
- ❋ A closure day – achieving excellence through valuing individuals; sharing the vision
- ❋ Children 'beyond' – pupils who challenge our hearts, minds and bodies!
- ❋ Raising self-esteem and morale of staff – reviewing and re-energising
- ❋ Parents and staff evenings – broadening the vision.

Train the trainers

Individuals delivering courses within our model should be accredited through a week-long intensive residential course. This course explains QCT and how to train others in its delivery. This training is fundamental to the success of QCT in a whole-school community. Without it QCT in school may lose its strength and purpose in your school.

Our website (**www.circle-time.co.uk**) includes testimonials from accredited trainers.

Additional courses from Jenny Mosley Consultancies

- ❋ Peer mediation
- ❋ Children 'beyond' – drugs education
- ❋ Bridging the circle – working on successful transition
- ❋ Boost your energy
- ❋ Switching children on to learning
- ❋ Relaxation training for all
- ❋ Children and staff
- ❋ NLP foundation skills
- ❋ Creative arts training days for all

- ☀ More than splish, splash, splosh
- ☀ Sound, move and make – integrating arts media
- ☀ Lifting the spirits
- ☀ The art of storytelling
- ☀ Power of puppets
- ☀ Bring drama into your Circle Time
- ☀ Developing a holistic approach to emotional health – creating the work–life balance
- ☀ Conference days
- ☀ After dinner speakers
- ☀ 'Train the trainers' for your own local education authority

For information about training, contact Jenny Mosley Consultancies:

Telephone: 01225 767157
E-mail: circletime@jennymosley.co.uk
Website: www.circle-time.co.uk
Address: 28A Gloucester Road, Trowbridge, Wiltshire, BA14 0AA

Books and resources

Mosley, J. (1993) *Turn your School Round*

Mosley, J. (1996) *Quality Circle Time*

Mosley, J. (1998) *More Quality Circle Time*

Mosley, J. (2006) *Using Rewards Wisely*

Mosley, J. and Sonnet, H. (2002) *101 Games for Self-Esteem*

Mosley, J. and Sonnet, H. (2002) *Making Waves*

Mosley, J. and Sonnet, H. (2003) *101 Games for Social Skills*

Mosley, J. and Sonnet, H. (2005) *Better Behaviour through Golden Time*

Mosley, J. and Sonnet, H. (2006) *101 Games for Better Behaviour*

Mosley, J. and Sonnet, H. (2006) *Helping Children Deal with Anger*

Mosley, J. and Sonnet, H. (2006) *Helping Children Deal with Bullying*

Mosley, J. and Sonnet, H. (2007) *Helping Children Deal with Conflict*

Mosley, J. and Thorp, G. (2005) *Positive Playtimes*

Mosley, J. (2000) *Quality Circle Time in Action*

Mosley, J. (2000) *Quality Circle Time Kit*

Mosley, J. (2004) *Reward Certificates*

Mosley, J. (2005) *Golden Rules Poster*

Mosley, J. (2005) *Lunchtimes Poster Set*

Mosley, J. (2005) *Playground Poster Set*

Mosley, J. (2005) *Playground Stars*

Mosley, J. (2007) *Stickers*

All these resources are published in Cambridge by LDA. For information about the full range of Jenny Mosley's books and resources, please contact LDA Customer Services on 0845 120 4776 or visit our website at **www.LDAlearning.com**

Appendix 1

Behavioural support for everyone through the Quality Circle Time model

The QCT model provides a sound platform of positive behavioural management along with emotional literacy support for all children. The major features of QCT include:

- ⁕ a self-care programme for teachers;
- ⁕ key listening systems;
- ⁕ the Golden Rules boundaries system;
- ⁕ an incentives system called Golden Time;
- ⁕ a sanctions system involving the loss of Golden Time;
- ⁕ an effective lunchtime and playtime policy;
- ⁕ special features for children beyond the usual strategies.

The model requires a commitment to holding regular circle times for children and staff. The energy and self-esteem of staff are key to getting everything in perspective and being able to succeed. When we are working with troubled children, this is especially important.

The checklist on page 166 enables you to find out if you have boundaries in place in your school.

Wave 1 and the Quality Circle Time model

We have worked with many schools that have embedded the QCT model in their policy. The model is underpinned by sound psychological theory, and it is ecosystemic. By this, we mean that it works with and permeates the entire school system. The model is well documented (see the books and resources section in Chapter 13) and it is not our intention to explain this system in full here. However, we feel that outlining some of the main features of the model's Wave-1 support will help those who want to set up a sound support system for children, before considering any child who may be beyond these strategies. We hope that this outline will help you to put the provision for children 'beyond' into perspective and to ensure that the number of children beyond the systems is kept to a minimum. We have provided a series of checklists on pages 167–169 to help you to assess in relation to your school the aspects of QCT covered in this appendix.

The Golden Rules to reinforce boundaries

The Golden Rules are a set of values that extend into every area of school life. They enable children to become more aware that their behaviour is their choice and that the many choices they make during the day can be influenced by the rules.

The Golden Rules we advocate are the following:

We are gentle	We don't hurt others
We are kind and helpful	We don't hurt anybody's feelings
We listen	We don't interrupt
We are honest	We don't cover up the truth
We work hard	We don't waste our own or others' time
We look after property	We don't waste or damage things

Posters displaying the Golden Rules may be obtained from LDA.

The use of Golden Time

Golden Time is a consistent and efficient system for celebrating success. It is structured to reinforce the Golden Rules and to enable children who keep these rules to have the opportunity of choosing a special activity during the week. A full description of the system can be found in *Better Behaviour through Golden Time* (see the books and resources section in Chapter 13). If children break a Golden Rule, they are given a warning. With older children we use a warning card for this. With younger children and those with special educational needs, we use a visual and interactive display of sun and cloud symbols – a child moves a clothes peg with their name on it between these, depending on their behaviour. If a child fails to heed a warning they may lose some of their Golden Time, although they are given a chance to earn their time back by correcting their behaviour.

Use the checklist on page 167 to assess whether your Golden Time is successful.

> *I've seen the concept of Golden Time in operation in schools I have visited and been impressed by the difference it makes. The Golden Rules are simple, common sense, but every teacher knows that ensuring every child abides by them in the modern world is a constant challenge.*
>
> David Blunkett, in the foreword to
> *Better Behaviour through Golden Time*

Tiny Achievable Tickable Targets

If a child struggles to access their Golden Time, they may need a structured set of academic and/or behavioural targets. We recommend the use of Tiny Achievable Tickable Targets (TATTs) that guarantee success and boost self-esteem. These are small, specific things for a child to work on in a given time-frame. Initially, this can be done in one, two or three 3-minute sessions in the morning, during which the child's target is an agreed standard of work or behaviour. Once the child succeeds, the standard can be raised or the time period extended. The aim is that the child might, in time, be able to access the Golden Time system fully.

Golden Time and serious offences

Golden Time is used differently for a serious offence. If a child is involved in a physical or serious verbal attack, having passed the warning stage, they lose ten minutes of Golden Time which cannot be earned back. The school's own serious-incident system would need to be followed – the child is likely to be reported to the headteacher, and the offence written in an incident book while the child witnesses this. This is usually signed by all parties concerned. The child's parents or carers are likely to be involved.

Whole-class targets and peer support

Sometimes the class egg on a child 'beyond'. The children might use them as a scapegoat to distract the teacher so that their own poor behaviour or work is overlooked. A good strategy is to make a child's tiny target – such as sitting calmly in their seat – a whole-class target. If everyone keeps the target, they could receive a little extra Golden Time or play a favourite game.

Quality listening systems

Schools need high-quality listening systems. Our whole-school model incorporates three listening systems: Quality Circle Time, Bubble Time and Think Time Books.

QCT is a highly structured weekly Circle Time that provides a listening system for everyone in the school. Children sit with their class teacher and other relevant adults to make decisions, solve problems and explore issues co-operatively. Moral values cannot be taught but are experienced, and this forum provides opportunities for this.

Bubble Time is a one-to-one listening system that provides an opportunity for a private discussion between the teacher and a pupil.

Think Time Books are offered to every child as a daily non-verbal way of communicating with the teacher.

Use the checklist on page 168 to assess your school's listening systems.

Promoting positive lunchtimes

Lunchtimes and playtimes may be the most contentious times of the school day. A stressful lunchtime or playtime may affect a child's ability to work and participate once they come back into the classroom. *Positive Playtimes* (see the books and resources section in Chapter 13) is a comprehensive guide to creating happy lunchtimes, and a useful source of playground games. In brief, strategies for positive lunchtimes and playtimes include:

- teaching playground games, first to supervisors and then to children;
- zoning the playground into activity areas;
- organising Playground Friends – a system of supervision by older children;
- community taskforces for children who need constructive activities;
- establishing a football parliament to ensure that football contributes to the positive ethos of the school, rather than acting against it;
- linking playground rules with the Golden Rules.

On page 169 there is a checklist to use in order to assess your lunchtimes and playtimes.

Checking that you have clear boundaries in place

	Yes	No	Action plan
Is there evidence of a whole-school approach to understanding moral values, such as displays, drawings, pictures and adverts created by children?			
Have parents received and signed two copies of the Golden Rules – one copy to keep and one to return to school?			
Are there photos of children keeping the Golden Rules displayed around the school with Golden Rules posters?			
Are the Golden Rules displayed in all such school areas as the classrooms, playground, corridors and dining hall?			
Is there evidence that all the children, teaching and non-teaching staff know about the Golden Rules? Do staff refer to them in their dealings with children?			
Do you use stickers saying 'Well done for keeping the Golden Rules'?			
Are the normal classroom routines – such as guidelines for lining up, tidying up and what to do if stuck – displayed and kept separately from the Golden Rules?			

Making sure you have a successful Golden Time system

	Yes	No	Action plan
Is Golden Time used as a special incentive for keeping the Golden Rules all week?			
Have you talked through your plans to use Golden Time with your headteacher, other teachers and the parents or carers of your class?			
Is Golden Time timetabled weekly for Key Stage 2 and daily for Key Stage 1?			
Have you sold the new system to the children? Do you use it as a celebration and talk about it positively?			
Have you a selection of good golden activities that the children can choose from? Children could discuss what they would like during Circle Time.			
Have you introduced some activities for the whole class that let older children play with younger children and others?			
Do all the children understand that if they break a Golden Rule they will receive a warning, and if they carry on breaking it they may lose some of their Golden Time?			
Is a record kept of the loss of Golden Time?			
Do you allow children to earn back Golden Time on your terms, not as part of an attention-seeking game by them?			
Does a child who loses Golden Time sit with a sand timer waiting to join in, in sight of the activity they want to do?			
Are Golden Time certificates sent home termly for all children who have kept the Golden Rules?			
Could you invite other people, like midday supervisors or members of the community, to Golden Time sessions?			

Permission to Photocopy

Checking that the Quality Circle Time listening systems are in place

	Yes	No	Action plan
Are the following three listening systems in place in school: Circle Time, Think Time Books and Bubble Time?			
Is Quality Circle Time timetabled?			
Does each class use a Circle Time kit bag (available from LDA)?			
Do you have books and resources to support your use of Quality Circle Time?			
Does your Circle Time practice include the use of metaphor, puppets and role play?			
Are the five skills of listening, looking, thinking, speaking and concentrating displayed in the school?			
Can a space be easily made available in the classroom for a circle of chairs for Circle Time?			
Do you use 'Do Not Disturb – Quality Circle Time in action' signs on your door(s) to avoid disturbance?			
Have the Circle Time rules been explained and linked to the Golden Rules?			
Is there a quiet place in the classroom where an adult can conduct Bubble Time?			

Making sure that lunchtimes and playtimes are good times

	Yes	No	Action plan
Are your midday supervisory assistants (MDSAs) trained in using the Golden Rules and the playground rules?			
Are MDSAs part of the incentives and sanctions system that operates school-wide?			
Are the Golden Rules and playground rules displayed in play areas?			
Is there a Playground Friends system, whereby trained teams of children who wear special hats or other symbols of their responsibility help other children in the playground?			
Are invitations given to MDSAs to attend assemblies and Circle Time sessions?			
Is the playground zoned to allow different activities to take place safely?			
Is there evidence of a 'craze of the week', such as skipping or clapping games, to support MDSAs in finding creative and fulfilling activities for the children?			
Are wet-play boxes available to provide extra support and activities when it is raining?			
Is there a wet-play system to help manage these potentially tricky days?			
Is there a well-managed football club with its own ground rules?			
Are there Friendship Stops on the playground to help combat loneliness?			
Do MDSAs have their own incentives system for the children?			

Appendix 2

Wave-3 support and beyond

Therapeutic support

There will be some children in school whose needs will be so severe and troubling that it will not be possible to meet them by using in-school intervention projects. If you have concerns about a child, it is best to take these to a staff Circle Time and talk them through. Talk to your SENCo, headteacher and behavioural support staff, and to the child's previous class teachers. It is important to ensure that everyone who works with the pupil is aware of what you are trying to do as a fragmented approach can cause more problems for you and the child.

There is no substitute for calling in a trained professional to support children who experience severe distress. Trained therapists receive support and supervision for their role. Teachers are rarely trained to carry out therapies, and they need to make sure that they do not take on more than can be managed. Most teachers have another thirty or so children in the classroom waiting for their time and attention, each with their own needs.

When providing extra support in school is not the answer

There comes a very difficult stage when, although a child is responding well to a Circle of Support, it might not be advisable for them to continue. You may be aware that you are merely putting a finger in the dam. In other words, there is just enough support to keep the child on track and provide a safety net, but the problem is not being tackled. If you reach this stage, you will need to discuss the best long-term approach with other staff involved. Primary schools are very good at keeping children going. In secondary school the same child often cannot cope with having eight different teachers in different settings, with a variety of teaching approaches. Keeping a child from the psychiatric support that they need in the primary-school setting may result in a bigger problem for them when they reach secondary school.

Involving local secondary schools is an important aspect of a successful Circle of Support programme. When a circle includes vulnerable children who are about to move on to secondary school, having a teacher from that school involved is invaluable. This will help to make the child's transition to the secondary school as smooth as possible. If the same teacher can continue to include the child in a Circle of Support at the new school, so much the better. However, this on its own will not be enough for children with the most severe problems.

When you feel that nothing is working

There may come a time when nothing seems to be helping a child. Spending all your time and energy looking after the child in question will sap your reserves, push you to your limits and deprive other children of your attention and of learning opportunities. At this point, your well-being and that of the other children and staff need to be protected. The other children in the class need to be made safe and a timetable of support should be drawn up to give teachers in this position a break.

When a child is not responding to any of your input, a very serious stage has been reached. The staff will need to agree that the consistent application of all previous strategies has failed and that this particular troubled and troubling child can no longer benefit from the current mainstream provision your school is offering. At this stage the emphasis must move from trying to support the child to caring for your sanity and the sanity of your colleagues. The headteacher will also need support during the arduous process of seeking additional support or a place for the child in a special education context.

The work of trained therapists

Superb work can be done in school to help children by providing psychotherapy, psychology, arts and creativity projects, drama, sports, music, relaxation, yoga and peer massage. However, professional therapeutic support should be supplied only by trained therapists who understand how to help children in these ways. It is beyond the scope of this book to go further into this. Suffice it to say that this appears to be a growing field and there are a lot of exciting projects to explore.

What can be done for the child who is beyond being 'beyond'?

The only way to assess such a child is by teachers and co-workers getting together at a staff meeting to discuss the child and the situation. Such staff meetings should be held every half-term. We have heard from teachers who have never been to staff meetings at which children are discussed. They discuss car-parking issues, the school fair, and art displays round the school, but the support of children with challenging behaviour may not even get on the agenda.